KICKING THE ODDS

Other Books By Shaun C. Kilgore

Heaven's Point Guard: The Kirk Gentrup Story (with Ken "Cruiser" Gentrup)

Remember The Ride: The Story Of North Vermillion Girls Basketball's Sensational Four-Year Run (with Ken "Cruiser" Gentrup)

Kicking
The Odds

Brett Sheldon &
Shaun C. Kilgore

FOUNDERS HOUSE PUBLISHING
2012

For information address Founders House Publishing, LLC,
Suite 200A 614 Wayne Street, Danville, IL 61832
www.foundershousepublishing.com

ISBN: 978-0-9843764-4-5

Book design: Shaun Kilgore
Cover Design: Shaun Kilgore
Background cover photo: copyright Greg Flint

All photos enclosed used with permission.
pg 16, Photo courtesy of Kdog PHOTOGRAPHERS
pgs 28, 76, and 160, copyright Doug's Studio
pgs 64, 88, copyright Greg Flint
pg 108 copyright Tina Vredenburgh
pg 149, courtesy of the Dr. Phil Show
pg 154, courtesy of the New Orleans Saints

Printed in the United States of America

I dedicate this book to all of those that have supported me, believed in me, cheered for me, coached me, inspired me, motivated me, challenged me, disciplined me, loved me, and even those that laughed at me, made fun of me, and doubted me, because it is all of you that have helped me to become the person I am today.

—Brett

For my wife, Amanda, my children, and for everyone who has encouraged me along the way.

—Shaun

Acknowledgements

I WOULD like to thank God for helping me realize that anything is possible through Him. I would like to thank my mom. We have been through a lot together. Thanks to all of my school teachers that have gone out of their way to help me, yet didn't treat me differently.

Also thanks to my best friends: Justin Krout, Rodney Carver, Cap Quirk, Mitch Downs, Anthony Vredenburg, Jake Cook, Thomas Robinson, Jesse Scott, Ryan Carver, and Cole Bowman.

To my stepfather Andy for everything he has done for me.

Thanks to Clay Rush for seeing something in me I had not seen yet.

Also thanks to all of my football coaches: Coach Bolin, Coach Trout, Coach Leonard, Coach Miles, Coach Brown, Coach Duncan, Coach Culp, and, of course, both Coach Carvers.

To all of my friends' parents and families for taking me in like I was their own son, thank you.

Thanks to my Duncan and Sheldon families for loving and supporting me.

Special thanks to Shaun Kilgore for making this book possible.

My apologies to anyone that I have forgotten. I love you all.

Table Of Contents

Foreword

I REMEMBER sitting down to a birthday dinner and receiving a most unexpected message from Brett Sheldon. His message said that he was interested in getting help writing a book about his life. It was quite a birthday present. I had been lucky so far, getting the chance to write a father's story about his son, a local story called *Heaven's Point Guard: The Kirk Gentrup Story*. I have to say that looking back, that book was a stepping stone for me. It was the first opportunity to write a true story, a story about an exceptional person and one that dealt with serious themes like life and death. It was also my first time writing about an athlete. That book received wonderful attention locally and I'm proud of what it has accomplished in the two years since it was published. Heaven's Point Guard's success and local reach was what brought it to Brett's attention.

He had heard about the book from a friend who lived in the Rockville, Indiana area. When it came to his own story, Brett Sheldon certainly had one that drew not just my attention as a writer, but had garnered wider exposure through an appearance on the nationally syndicated talk show, The Dr. Phil Show.

When Brett sent that message I immediately read up on him, looking at his Facebook page, and searched Google. As many of you will find out reading the pages of this book, *Kicking The Odds*, Brett has overcome a lot of stigmas and preconceptions to become an accomplished individual. His successes as a football kicker at the high school and collegiate level naturally take on a very unique character when you consider Brett's birth defect. Despite his lack of full-length arms, he has excelled and made a place for himself in sports and in life.

Kicking The Odds shares many of the trials and triumphs that Brett Sheldon has experienced in his life. They are also meant to be examples of overcoming obstacles and taking hold of the opportunities that life has for you. His life is an inspiring example of what people can do if they simply set their minds to it. Much of what we think is impossible is really very possible. Just ask Brett.

The writing of this book has been an enjoyable collaboration in which I was able to meet and spend time with both Brett and his mother Laura, and hear many of these stories first-hand.

After spending the last several months helping Brett bring this story to life, I have to say that I'm encouraged and feel very privileged to have taken a part in sharing his thoughts and memories with all of you. I hope you enjoy reading *Kicking The Odds*.

It is my hope that you're inspired, that you're motivated by this young man's journey. It has been a long road, certainly, but the future is filled with bright promise and the opportunities are still there even if you don't see them at first. You must believe in yourself and believe that just about anything is possible.

Shaun C. Kilgore
Danville, Illinois
March 2012

"You measure the size of the accomplishment by the obstacles you had to overcome to reach your goals."

—Booker T. Washington

Introduction:
Seizing Opportunities

The first time I heard the words "Brett, get warmed up" was in the second quarter of our eighth game of the season against South Dakota State. I was a second-string kicker behind player Cory Little for Indiana State University waiting for the chance to have my debut on the field. It had been a difficult road getting here to this moment. After high school, I had started out at Franklin College as a freshman, and then transferred to Purdue University my sophomore year. I failed to get on the team during a walk-on attempt, so I ended up not playing football at all that entire year. Disappointed and a bit depressed, I questioned what I was doing for a while. In time, I made a final transfer to Indiana State and succeeded in making the team during another walk-on.

Now I had my moment. However, I hadn't attempted a kick in a game since my freshman year at Franklin. I was understandably nervous considering I had been out of football for well over a year. My apprehension was there but I knew I had to go ahead with it. There was no way I was missing this opportunity. I had come so far.

In the second quarter, Coach Trent Miles came up to me and said, "Next kick is yours." So I went over to the kicking net and started to warm up. A couple of minutes later we scored a long touchdown. It was time. I was jogging out on the field to try my first Division One attempt. I can only imagine what the other team was thinking when they saw me come out. Some of their fans or players were probably wondering if I had my arms in my shoulder pads. Those who had heard of me were probably telling those who hadn't. It wasn't like I was unfamiliar with the attention. It had followed me in one form or another since the first time I stepped out onto a playing field, and really my whole life.

I remember getting lined up seven yards behind the ball and trying to recall everything, every word of instruction and comment that my trainer, Clay Rush, used while he taught me about kicking technique. Preparing for the PAT, I stood there picturing the ball sailing right down the middle of the uprights. Clay had always taught me to know the kick was going to be good before I kicked it. In those brief moments I attained the kind of certainty that comes with knowing and trusting my capabilities as an athlete. You could say I was "in the zone." The next instant, the ball was snapped, and I started my steps. I kept my head down—plant foot was in perfect position—then snapped my leg forward and followed through. The kick went right down the middle. The crowd roared and gave us a standing ovation. The point I scored gave the team a 20-3 lead.

By the end, we won our fifth game of the season, beating South Dakota State 41-30. This was a great achievement because Indiana State football had been in decline over the last few years. They had won just a single game the season before and none the two seasons before that. I knew the work that Coach Miles had accomplished. He had done a commendable job turning the program around and getting it on the right track. I could say that I witnessed the great turnaround he had for the University. It was one of the most memorable opportunities in my life, but hardly the only one.

EACH OF us who are born into this world is given certain opportunities in life. Some are dictated by factors like position in society or our particular circumstances of birth. Others are based on the means and resources of the family we were born to. There are opportunities that are presented to us by others or by form of daily life in general. At some point, with so much available to us, it becomes essential to recognize that if you want to benefit from them you need to be ready to seize them. So many times, an opportunity presents itself but we fail to act. I do not exempt myself from that. I don't think anybody takes advantage of every one that crosses his or her path. It's part of being human to miss out sometimes.

For me, life has presented the sort of challenges that I used to sharpen or hone my ability to recognize and go after the things that I wanted. I admit now and will mention later that I've been influenced and flourished in competition. As an athlete it is a cornerstone, but I know that such a quality has helped to guide and shape the course of my life. It is my attitude, focused on success and shaped by struggle, which continues to lead me forward.

This book, *Kicking The Odds*, is about my journey so far and the sort of lessons I've learned along the way about engaging life on my own terms. I hope that what

I say along the way might encourage those who have faced their own adversities and trials. I also desire that the stories and lessons in these pages inspire others to stand up and seize opportunities in their own lives. I worked hard to overcome physical limitations, and worked even harder to dispel the perceived limitations that have been placed on me by other people. That is something everyone can relate to on some level.

No matter what has happened in your life, you will be confronted time and again by challenges that will make you question what it is you're doing or what you are pursuing. In these moments is where your attitude and mindset matter the most. I'm sure most of you understand that on some level already. It is something that is common to everyone. Still, are you ready to act? Are you ready to take on the challenges and persevere? Are you willing to put in the time and make the commitments that help you achieve what it is you want out of life regardless of what obstacles you might stumble over as you go? I have answered those questions again and again over the years. I've made the choices and put in the time.

In *Kicking The Odds*, I want to share my story with you. I hope you will read along and get a bit of encouragement. You might see some of the choices I've made and the opportunities that depended on other people and get some sense of where your circumstances are similar. I don't know. Keep reading then let me know what you think.

"I always felt that my greatest asset was not my physical ability, it was my mental ability."

—Bruce Jenner

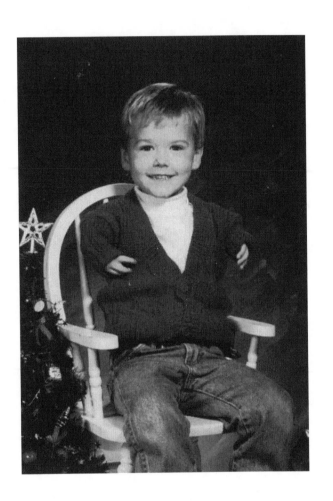

1
Hey 'No Arms!'

I REMEMBER at age six being so excited to go on my first bus ride. At that time, my mother and I were living in a small apartment in Crawfordsville, Indiana. It was my first day of kindergarten at John Beard Elementary School. Starting school was one of those first milestones, an introduction to a new world of possibilities to grow. For me, all of the details of that day remain sharp and distinctive. I remember my mother helping me get ready for school, gathering up the supplies I would need, and carefully arranging them in my backpack, then making me a quick breakfast.

When the big, yellow bus pulled up outside, even now I can recall the mixture of emotions. I was both excited and nervous at the same time. I'm not sure what sort of expectations I had at that age, but I know I had plenty of reasons to be wary. Still, I bravely walked to the bus, climbed aboard, and took a seat by a window, right in front of two boys I should have avoided. It didn't take long for my suspicions to be confirmed. In no time, these two boys, strangers to me at that point, were whispering in my ear as the bus continued to roll down the road.

"Hey, no arms," one of them said.

"Look at him, he has no arms," said the other.

Then they laughed. It seemed like the whole bus was laughing at me. I tried my best to hold back the tears, staring out the window of the bus while they gathered in my eyes. Heat rushed to my cheeks. It wasn't entirely embarrassment. I was angry. I didn't know how to express it, but I remember thinking that I would show them one day. I promised myself that I would not let the names, the whispers, or the laughter bring me down. I said to myself that it wouldn't be like this for long. Even then, I was an optimistic kid. I was right. I left Crawfordsville behind when my mother moved us back to her old stomping grounds in Fountain County, Indiana the following year. I took that experience with me and the promise I made to myself helped me going forward. While my circumstances did not improve immediately and certainly all of those things continued to be a part of my life, I had hope.

FOR AS long as I can remember, it was just my mom and I. Our life together was one of motion. From the apartment in Crawfordsville to one in Veedersburg, Indiana, and so on, we moved several times when I was young. I recognized that life does not guarantee stability or security for any of us. Over the course of my life I believe I've learned that lesson very well.

I'm sure that many of you can relate to what being in a divorced family is like. You have to go see your father or mother every other weekend; life seems like a juggling act where you don't know where to land the ball. In my case, I did not always feel so comfortable going to see my father. In some ways, he remained like a stranger to me. My parents had gotten divorced when I was only one year old. I had no memories of them being together. It was a struggle. Living with a single mom plus being born with this disability, this birth defect, which can never go unnoticed, was a struggle. It was always there for everyone to see, to make fun of, or at least point out. But it was the words, spoken in a whisper behind my back that affected me the most in the early years. I worked hard to use the callous words

11

of others to my advantage, to use it to fuel my ambitions and my competitiveness.

It was all so unexpected. Throughout my mom's pregnancy there had been no indications of a birth defect, nothing to fly up a red flag to the doctors. Everyone found out the day I was born. My arms had not developed the way they should. They were stunted. My hands had partially developed, providing me with three fingers on each hand. (The technical term is bilateral radial agenesis of the upper extremities.) I know it was a lot for my mom to absorb. She accepted what couldn't be changed and she loved me. Her acceptance, her belief in me, was forged from that day forward.

WHEN MY mother moved us to a little apartment in Veedersburg, Indiana, I was skeptic. I was still struggling with my bad experiences at Crawfordsville. As we were settling in, my mother told me I would be attending the same elementary school she attended, Southeast Fountain Elementary. When the day arrived, my first bus ride went much better. This time I didn't have anyone heckling me all the way to school. Sure, I still noticed the stares, but I look at it this way: It is to be expected when young children see something new or out of the ordinary. Perhaps, I could say the same thing for adults, but there is more to it than that.

People have expectations. It is a given for just about anybody. Sometimes, though, there are those who see something like my physical condition and put undue limitations on what I can be expected to do. They make a judgment based, in part, on their own experiences. When a person born with arms and legs fully developed sees me they might immediately think, "Well, he can't do this, he can't do that, and so on." Now, in some cases, they were dead wrong and I proved as much to them. I changed their perspectives—I hope for the better. Other times, I have encountered people who could see that with me there was more than meets the eye. One of those people was my first grade teacher Mrs. Derf.

This woman had been a teacher for a long time. She was a veteran of the school system and I found out that she taught my mother in elementary. Part of what was better about moving to Veedersburg was encountering this wise woman. She was somebody who saw past what I lacked physically to the person beneath. Mrs. Derf treated me the same way she treated other students. Looking back, I have tremendous respect for what she did as a teacher and how she treated me. I won't ever forget that. Thankfully, she was the first of many people who had vision and believed I had as much potential as the next person. That was crucial for me going forward.

Then there was Mrs. Fruits, my physical education teacher, who to this day tells the story about me in the first grade asking her to play catch with me because the other students were not as advanced as me in throwing the ball back, which I thought was neat she remembered that story after all of these years.

That same year, I met someone else who looked at me and just saw Brett, not a handicapped person, or the strangeness of my lack of arms. His name was Rodney Carver. He was, and continues to be, one of my best friends. Friendship, especially the kind that lasts, is something special. I've been lucky to have a small group of true friends that see me for who I am. Rodney was the first one. You can't really know what it meant to me to have somebody befriend me despite what was plain to see. Such friendships provided another building block in my life that helped me succeed. Honestly, friends can make or break you. If you have the wrong people in your life you might be worse off than if you'd never met them. Better still if you can be a friend to somebody else, and I mean the kind that encourages and builds up. Then you've accomplished something noble and valuable. I benefited from Rodney's friendship and others could benefit from yours. An understanding person who can step beyond cruel names and foolish comments is worth more than I can say. Just my opinion, I know, but give it a shot. You might be surprised.

WORDS CAN hurt. I titled this chapter with just one of the names I've been called over the years. It was the first one that really hit hard and stuck in my memory. I've learned to laugh at the names, even looked at them as terms of affection from friends who called me "six" or "musket." While the names have died down in many cases, the comments and the looks continue. I will talk about the ways I've dealt with that and maybe you'll see something there that could help you too. I'm happy if that's the case. There is no excuse to be limited and defined by such unfair and inaccurate views and closed mindsets. Each of us, regardless of our limits, has value. That's something to stand up for, something to support more than ever.

My mom and me

"Never let the fear of striking out get in your way."

—George Herman "Babe" Ruth

2
You Want To Play What?

I TALK a lot about expectations and how I have worked hard to transcend the low expectations that others have placed on me because of my physical differences. Yet there were people in my life who told me, either in words or actions, that I was capable of more than even I could imagine, and I was just as good as anybody else. Entering second grade, I had no idea that I was going to discover something that would change my life for the better.

At the time, I was making some new friends, including Cap Quirk, another lifelong friend. I realized that I was interested in doing the same activities that they were involved in. I was stubborn enough to see the potential in myself to do just what I set my mind to doing. My friends were involved in athletics and it seemed like so much fun. I had no idea that these first, hesitant steps would ignite my lifelong love of sports.

The object of my interest at the time was baseball, and little league baseball specifically. Soccer and football would come later. From the second grade through the sixth grade I dedicated myself to the game, but before I ever stepped foot on the diamond, I came to my mother with a request.

I remember arriving home and telling my mom I wanted to play baseball. I won't forget what she said at first.

"You want to play what?"

There was this look of shock or perhaps fear in her eyes. She was my mother. She wanted to protect me and she was afraid that I would get hurt or I would be disappointed. I'm sure she felt a whole bunch of different emotions.

For my part, I was a very persistent little boy. I couldn't tell you how many times I begged her to let me play. Tens or hundreds of times, I'm sure. I wasn't about to give up on my dream.

A point came when I remember her telling someone, "Who am I to tell my son he can't do something?" My mom believed in me. She could always see the potential in me and overcame her own apprehension to support me. Once the matter of permission was settled, it was time to find out whether I could have a chance to play.

Again, I was very fortunate in that my friend Rodney's father, Jeff Carver, was not only very involved in his athletic career but also happened to be the head coach of the local little league team in Hillsboro. Additionally, my mother knew the Carver family. She had gone to school with them. She called Rodney's dad to discuss the idea of me playing for his team. Jeff Carver gave me an opportunity; he let me on the baseball team.

When I started playing little league baseball, I don't think anyone expected much out of me. Again, they only saw what lacked on the outside. I was determined to show them otherwise. In fact, I became a very good ballplayer. I remember getting the smallest glove I could find so I could show the other players (and the spectators) that I could throw and catch with the best of them. Jeff took a leap of faith and gave me the opportunity to pitch too. I rounded out my game by also becoming a decent batter as well, a fact that might be hard for some people to imagine without me demonstrating.

Needless to say, I had an eventful second grade year. So much had happened in my life so far. It was a successful time for me. We were fortunate enough to win our league's baseball championship that year. I have to say that the success I had in the game got me hooked on competition. I slept with my first trophy for an entire week following that big win.

Many people now saw that my lack of full-length arms did not mean I was somehow incapable of playing alongside those who did. It was a great personal victory in that sense. I had proven something to myself too. The feeling of winning, the excitement and pride I felt, all came together. I believed I was on the right track and that the future was brighter because I had stepped out. In time, I came to understand that things in life do not always add up so clearly. There were plenty of bumps on the road ahead.

AT THE beginning of my third grade year there were some changes in my personal life that didn't so much affect me negatively as they gave me a new perspective and the chance to spend time with my grandparents.

My mother had been working as a hairdresser locally, but had applied and then accepted a job as a flight
attendant in order to better care for the both of us. The
only trouble was that she was out of town a lot. The so-
lution came when we moved to my grandparents'
home. Jesse and Wilma Rogers had adopted my mother
and were the best grandparents I could have asked for.
Grandma was a tough German woman who never hesi-
tated to speak her mind when it was necessary. She
could offer an opinion on just about anything. Honestly, she could be intimidating to some people. In contrast, my grandfather was more even-tempered and rather sweet. He would do just about anything for us.
They both took me in when my mother had to fly out.

One thing I remember clearly about that time was
that I learned a lot about being disciplined and trying
very hard to be well behaved when I was with them,
especially when I was around Grandma Wilma. I remember getting in trouble and being chased around the
house. She was wielding a small twig she'd pulled from
one of the trees and was determined to switch me good.
Of course, when I ran outside and she couldn't catch
me she just locked the door and waited for grandpa to
come. My grandma could be sort of scary when she
was angry. My living arrangements made things interesting but all went fairly well.

At school, another excellent teacher named Mrs. Krout had a great impact on my life. She showed me the same sort of tolerance and compassion and a willingness to go beyond what she could see to what was beneath the surface. I was grateful for that then and still am today.

That same year, I met Justin Krout. (No relation to my teacher.) We became closer friends and remain the same today. I remember that he used to carry my lunch for me at school and helped me with anything I asked. I now had three close friends and we spent a lot of time together, sometimes on the baseball field.

That part of my life continued to improve as well. I was enamored by the game of baseball and had only gotten better as I stretched myself and grew more confident in my own physicality. We played a good season in little league and ended up winning another championship.

Baseball gave me a way to focus my mind and my talents in a positive way. I know that the training, discipline, and the hard work involved in that sport began to build something in me. Today, I still carry even the earliest lessons that playing on that little league team provided me. They informed my future progress as an athlete and as a person.

All in all, certain aspects of my life continued to get better. Was everything perfect? No, of course not. I didn't see my mother as much as I would have liked. She was putting herself out there, doing what she had to do to provide for the both of us. Undoubtedly she was under many strains and pressures I could only guess at now and certainly didn't consider when I was so young. My mom believed in me and let me step out to see what I could be capable of. She provided me with an opportunity and I jumped on it.

"Do what you can, with what you have, where you are."

—Theodore Roosevelt

3

A Sport You Don't Need Arms For

AT THIS point in my childhood I think I was finding a place where I belonged, where I could express myself and test my abilities. Athletics, the competitive atmosphere, and the physical challenges all played a part in helping me realize what I could do. I loved playing baseball. The game gave me so much at that young age that I wasn't sure if there was another place where I could find I could belong.

The year I entered the fourth grade, my mom announced that she had found a place to rent and that we were moving. The strange irony was that the house she

29

found in the tiny town of Newtown, Indiana was owned by my uncle—my father's twin brother. Unlike previous moves, this new one wasn't even a problem for me. I would still be going to the same school at Fountain Central. I wouldn't have to make any new friends. My mom was adamant about keeping me in the same school district and providing more stability. I wouldn't have to start over again. That was important really. I realized that beyond the game of baseball, I had dear friends and close relationships I didn't want to lose. There were also benefits to Newtown too. While I had liked living with my grandparents for the most part, the fact that they lived in a nearly isolated country house had worn on me some. I was a bit rambunctious and thrived more when I was able to spend time with other kids my age. Plus, I did like the change of scenery too.

While settling into my new home, my mom did something that I don't think she realized would affect my life so dramatically. What did she do? It seemed like a simple thing: she signed me up for a soccer league in Covington, Indiana, a town located just west of Veedersburg. I jumped at the opportunity to try a new sport that almost seemed like a natural fit for somebody who lacked full arms. You didn't need arms or hands to play soccer. You just needed a good pair of legs and you needed to be quick on your feet. I think I had that covered.

When the day approached for me to go to the first practice, all of the old doubts and fears filled the back of my mind. I wondered whether the kids in Covington would accept me right away. I thought about this in a couple of ways. First, they'd never seen my arms. Second, they were a rival school. So there might be some conflict. I had a strong feeling it would be a big challenge and I was right.

During that first practice, I felt so out of place. I noticed that some of the other guys seemed to think they were somehow better than everyone else. They were a conceited bunch. They didn't have much sympathy for me, even though I was a new player, and hadn't any time to really practice or gain skill in the game. If they weren't yelling at me every time I made a mistake, they simply pretended I didn't exist. It was frustrating for a while, but I held on. I didn't quit. I stayed at it, learning and getting better. I was under a personal challenge to show them what I could do given just the chance. Later that year, I helped our soccer team win a championship. I achieved a level of respect and developed a love of soccer that first rivaled my love of baseball but quickly supplanted it.

I never thought another sport would take its place. Of course, I was wrong. Many things were fitting into place that year. I was young enough to still be caught up in childish wonder and I had more than my fair share of enthusiasm. I carried it into soccer for another two years before the game of football entered my life.

I WANT to underscore again that I stepped out into a new direction because there was someone there who believed in me. I mean, I was bursting with confidence and a deep desire to prove myself, but there was still someone outside who took an interest and brought any opportunity to my attention. In the case of soccer, it was my mom who came to me. That itself is ironic too when you think about how much a stretch my playing baseball seemed to her at the time. Maybe she saw soccer as a means for me to concentrate and showcase the strengths I had physically. I don't know. Perhaps, it doesn't matter why. The point is that I got that chance.

Opportunities, no matter how they come, are not always recognized for what they truly are or what sort of changes they can bring to our lives. I certainly had no idea that soccer would lead me to football and football would bring about other opportunities—both on and off the field.

AT THE same time all of this was going on in my life, there were changes in my mom's life too—the kind of changes that affected us both for the better and opened me up to some new experiences and broadened my understanding of discipline and focus.

You see, my mom met a man named Andy Duncan who later became my stepfather. Andy had a reputation as a hard-working farmer and was well respected in the local community. I was ten years old at this time and had been without a father figure for most of my life. Despite the fact that my father had lived a mere forty-five minutes away in Lafayette, Indiana, and I saw him every other weekend, I could not say we were very close at that time. Later on, we did work on our relationship and it grew as I got older.

Living with a single mother who was struggling to make ends meet was not something either of us wanted anymore. When my mother started dating Andy, I was not very optimistic about the situation. I didn't expect it would go anywhere. Although my mom had remained single the majority of my life up to that point, she did have a few serious relationships, but they just didn't work out. I do have to say that among the few relationships she did have, there were some pretty decent guys.

I don't remember a lot about her boyfriend Colby because I was so young, but she has always told me about how wonderful he and his family were to me. She said they took me in and accepted me as their own. They were a good family and we were blessed to have them in our lives.

I was older when she met Jason. She met him while working for the airline and they maintained a long distance relationship for a while. He was from Bermuda and we came very close to moving there. I remember my first trip over there with my mom, and his entire family was wonderful and also accepting. Although it didn't work out, they remain friends today. It is funny how things work out because if we had actually moved there, I probably would have been focused entirely on soccer. I don't believe football would have been an option. Regardless, my mom and I were really fortunate to have them in our lives as well.

When she started dating Andy, things seemed different. He continued to come around and gradually the two of them grew closer. At some point, I'm not sure when, Andy asked my mother and I to move in with him.

We moved to a house just a few miles out side of Veedersburg, not a serious move at all. Out on the farm now, I was encouraged by Andy and my mother to take an interest in 4-H. Both had been involved in the program as children and they believed it would teach me more about responsibility. I remember trying to decide the kind of animal I would be showing in the county fair. Andy was a cattle farmer so cows were in abundance. Yet, I knew working with such a large animal would be too difficult for me. Instead, we thought swine would be the best option. My mother had showed swine as a young girl. Pigs were much easier to show—at least I thought they were.

Soon enough, I understood that there was a lot involved in showing pigs. First, you had to guide them around with a whip, tapping them with it when you needed them to move. It might sound cruel, but if they are well trained you barely need to touch them at all. I had to walk them for an hour every night for the two months leading up to the fair in order to get them show-ready. Believe me, if you didn't take that time, those pigs would do something to embarrass you in the ring. The judges and the crowd will be able to tell how much attention you gave them.

Something amazing happened my first year in 4-H. My mother and Andy talked me into doing the showmanship part of the fair. In this section, you are judged according to how competently you show the swine in the ring. You are judged in a number of ways. You have to maintain eye contact with the judge, keeping the animal between you and him, your knowledge of the breed, etc. Additionally, they noted how you guided the pig, whether you struck too hard or were able to guide it with ease.

On that day, I had the chance to watch an advanced competition prior to my turn in the ring. I monitored every detail of the performance. Once it ended, I was up. I took my pig out through the gate. As the competition carried on, I got excited because I was one of three contestants that remained in the running. As the judge went into great detail for what he was looking for, I noticed him walking my way. As he reached out his hand I heard him say, "Congratulations," and the crowd cheered as the judge shook the hand of the boy beside me. Though I did not win intermediate showmanship the first time, I did just a few years later. I won Grand Champion with my crossbred barrow about five years after this. 4-H was a fun and successful time for me. Without Andy in my life, that opportunity would have never happened for me.

OPPORTUNITIES MAY be something we have to seize with all our strength or they might drift lightly into our hands because of the actions of others. You can never know exactly what kind will come your way. What makes the most difference is being aware of the possibilities and having the willingness to accept them when they arrive. I can't stress how much attitude has to do with this.

I'll be the first to admit that attitude is more a work-in-progress than a settled thing, but it is crucial to recognize how your attitude might illuminate opportunities or blind you to them.

Me with my first champion trophy in 4-H

"*Obstacles don't have to stop you. If you run into a wall, don't turn around and give up. Figure out how to climb it, go through it, or work around it.*"

—Michael Jordan

4
Two Ways To Kick

EVERYONE MAKES choices in life. It seems we are always weighing different options that come into our paths and if we're smart we try to weigh the consequences of one way versus another. This is true no matter whether you're a child of ten or thirty-year old adult. The difference lies in the wisdom you've gained from making bad decisions and the unexpected opportunities that may have resulted from picking one thing over another. You might think this a matter of common sense. For most people it is that, but when you've faced other adversities or had to overcome physical obstacles due to certain disabilities, it takes on some significance, at least in your own mind.

I don't want anyone to think that just because I was born the way I was and I had to suffer in certain ways that I deserve more credit for what choices I've made that have ultimately benefitted me. No matter who you are, when you have to make important choices it helps to have a bit of courage to step out in unexpected directions. I'm not saying that just because you've done well at something that when another opportunity comes up to do something else that you should automatically abandon the path you were on. It's never that simple. You can't know every consequence. It might be better to stick with what you've been doing. That is the power of choices. They can literally change your life. And sometimes not in positive ways.

I think it might be best to illustrate this point by talking about soccer. You see I became a tremendous soccer player during fifth and sixth grade and I remained attached to baseball as well. You already read how my mom got me involved on a soccer team in a nearby town. I'm still so thankful she went out of her way to take me to all of the soccer and baseball practices at this age. I know she didn't have to do all that. It was a sacrifice that I know some parents of disabled children may not have made. Unfortunately, they might not believe in their child's capacity to be involved like other so-called normal kids.

I had trials learning the game of soccer. I had the low expectations of my fellow players and the people at large as factors to overcome. I mean you can only imagine how some of them reacted to me. It's strange at times to reflect back on it as an adult. Children can be both extremely receptive and welcoming to differences as well as terribly cruel. The contrast could be severe. These were the sorts of experiences that shaped who I am.

Despite all of it, I excelled. I helped the soccer team win a championship while also helping to take the baseball team to another championship. It was all pretty impressive to me then. Yet, it also foreshadowed my future in athletics and what I would accomplish on a very different field.

The colorful remarks and awkward glances tapered off once I started showing people what I could do. I grew to enjoy soccer very much. In fact, I had thought it would have been great moving to Covington to play at the high school level. However, that was a path I did not take.

In fifth grade, I think my mom really grasped my real potential and wanted me to get out and play soccer at other areas as well. She signed me up in an indoor league in Lafayette. I played a season there and I was elected MVP of the league. After a successful time in the league, another team's coach that I played against later asked me to join a soccer team that he had put together which included a number of Lafayette kids. The coach's name was Dr. Robert Hagen. He was an orthopedic surgeon. We heard about him because of his work treating the injuries of athletes in our area.

It's amazing at the connections you can make if you just put yourself out there and go for it. You have to be willing to seize those opportunities. I have made so many friends through athletics and I wouldn't take it back for anything.

I ended up playing on Dr. Hagen's soccer team for about three years. We won a tournament or two but I knew eventually I would have to choose. I had to weigh the options. On the outset, I think I might have considered moving in order to continue playing soccer, which was at that time my best sport. I felt that I could go pretty far in soccer. I had friends at Fountain Central but I wasn't sure what else it offered me.

In all honesty, when I started the sixth grade, it was like my question had been answered for me. My friends were excited about playing football. Initially, I had no interest in playing at all. I had serious doubts about my ability to engage in the game. I couldn't see myself being very effective while wearing those big shoulder pads. In the end, though, my friends talked me into signing up. After all, I wasn't going to sit around and do nothing while my friends were having fun!

I think my friends helped me see that my background in soccer and my skill kicking the ball could be useful in football. I also believe the sixth grade football coach had an inkling of my ability too. The coach knew I could kick a ball really well since he had witnessed my skills during recess. This convinced him to set up a field goal team at the end of every practice for me to try.

I know what you're thinking: Most teams at that age do not kick any type of extra points or field goals, especially soccer style, which is the recommended way to kick field goals. Kicking with your toe is less accurate. The fact was that I hit extra points consistently in the sixth grade. As far as I know, we were the only team who did. This opened many people's eyes. I was laying the groundwork for my future in football and didn't really know it at that time. I still loved soccer and tried to stay involved.

During my first year in football, we had four small scrimmages and I ended up at 5/6 on PATs. I think the only scrimmage our team lost in the sixth grade was against Seeger, a rival school. I remember a series of jamboree games where I spent a lot of time anxious to do something, anything. I was one energetic kid and had gotten bored waiting to show everybody what I could do with the ball. When the second jamboree game began, I remember our coach telling the opposing team's coach that we were going to kick after we scored. I remember the first time I went out on the field to kick. The other team was a bit stunned when I came out. I proceeded to hit four out of five kicks that day. It was just the beginning for me. I realized I wanted to get better at kicking that football and determined that I would do just that. I wanted to be five for five. When the season ended I planned to spend the entire off-season practicing my kicking skills. I was going to be the best seventh grade kicker in the state. I now had two ways to kick and I spent part of my seventh grade year trying to choose between the two sports.

I WAS very nervous going into the seventh grade. Would I be cool? Would I make the grades? Our school was an integrated Jr. High and high school. That meant you could be a seventh-grader and walk by a senior in the halls. When the year began I was still juggling football and soccer. I would go to the football practice and immediately have to go over to Covington for soccer. I was considering playing soccer at Covington High School, which would mean no Mustang football for me.

I still had another year or two to decide, so at this point I was enjoying life, having the best of both worlds.

Football had been such an eye opening experience the previous year and I knew that I could actually be a successful kicker and I knew I wanted to continue the journey. Slowly, but surely, football was taking first place in my mind.

A funny story that comes to mind when I think about junior high football involves the very first practice. I was in our stretching lines with the team when one of our coaches, Coach Culp, walked by and gave me a funny look. He asked me, "Where are your arms." He seemed to think I had them tucked into my shoulder pads. The only reply I could think of was, "I'm the kicker." It's funny because I can't tell you how many times people have walked by me on the street and asked if I was cold because they thought my arms were tucked into my shirt.

When it comes to those things, you do your best to make the best of it, I think. Making a place in football required adjustments for not just me but for others as well.

I REMEMBER one game from seventh grade football that most of you would sooner forget than cherish, but

I can see it was a learning experience as all failures can be if you have the right perspective.

It was our last game of the year and we were playing at North Vermillion. It was a very boring game, especially from a kicker's perspective. The game was scoreless. We were 0-0 with only a couple of minutes left. It seemed we were driving the ball down the field quite willingly.

I remember being very excited I might get the opportunity to win the game for us with a field goal. As we got closer I started to get warmed up. We had all of our timeouts left and used them after every play until we got the ball in my field goal range. (I was able to kick a thirty-yard field goal in the seventh grade.) With 10 seconds left we ran one more play and called a time out with 3 seconds left. We were on the right hash about 26 yards out. Going out there, it was my first field goal attempt ever. Most of you probably may be thinking, "But you said you went five for six last year?" Yes, but those kicks were extra points, which are much easier than field goals, especially a field goal from a hash.

I trotted out on the field, ready to win the game. The ball was snapped and the kick was up. I looked up to watch the ball sail wide right of the field goal post. I had never been taught how to kick from a hash before.

I kicked the ball straight instead of angling it a bit to the left. Though I failed to hit that winning field goal, we tied the game 0-0 and the season was over. I could have let it deter me from football. I could have run back to soccer.

Instead, I realized I needed help to become the kind of kicker I believed I could be. One of the results of that first year was a surprising gift from Coach Bolin, the head varsity coach. At the time, Fountain Central replaced the goal posts and they were going to discard them. Bolin asked me if I wanted one. Andy had it placed in our yard.

That same year, I met a man who would change my life. His name was Clay Rush.

Old goal posts from Fountain Central High School in my yard

"The difference between a successful person and others is not lack of strength, not a lack of knowledge, but rather a lack of will."

—Vince Lombardi

Me with Clay Rush during a summer training visit

5

Clay Rush

FOLLOWING THE early developments during my seventh grade season, my mom and Andy recognized that I had some real potential in football and chose to help me develop the kind of skills I would need to be more competent and successful as a kicker. I was excited about the prospect of moving forward in a new sport and I knew it would present some new challenges for me both mentally and physically. I have always ran headlong into those sort of situations, using the constraints to drive my ambitions—my desire to prove that I was just as capable as anyone else. I also knew that I was hitting limits to my practical knowledge or even my ability to improve my performance. I needed help and my mom and Andy were determined to find it.

Soon, they were doing research to find local football camps that were operating around the area. The closest camp they found was being held at Purdue University—forty miles north in Lafayette, Indiana. The prestigious university was hosting the Pelfrey Kicking Camp. The camp was held over two days and I joined other young players for two four-hour sessions.

I remember walking into Purdue's indoor football facility and realizing that I was, by far, the youngest kid there that day. I felt a bit unnerved by the fact that the majority were probably juniors and seniors in high school, many of whom were looking to get recruited by the college. There were even some college-aged players there. I was lucky enough to meet someone closer to my age at the camp. His name was Kyle. The main thing I noticed was that he was being helped by a very tall man who could kick the ball twice as far as I could. That man was named Clay Rush.

Once I was introduced to Clay, he started in on me too, testing my skills and just seeing what I could do before he agreed to do anything else. The first thing I remember him doing was setting up a ball at the extra point. He told me to show him what I could do with it. Without hesitation, I hit the ball through.

Clay looked at me. "You have a good leg. I think we just need to work on your form."

That was the beginning of my friendship with Clay Rush. He seemed to see past my physical disability to my true potential. In a way, Clay took me under his wing, mentoring me and helping me gain better skills as a kicker. We continued to work together for the next few years. You might be wondering who he is. Let met tell you a bit about him.

Clay Rush was an outstanding place kicker. He attended Missouri Western State University where he made the All-Conference team all four years and made All-American as a senior. After school, Clay secured a contract playing in the AFL, or the Arena Football League, where he remained for ten years. First, he started with the Iowa Barnstormers. Next, he moved to the New York Dragons, then the Indiana Firebirds. In 2007, Clay played for Kansas City and Arizona. Finally, he ended his career with the Colorado Crush. He was named kicker of the year by the AFL in both 2000 and 2003.

I remember seeing him on game highlights while watching ESPN. The reporter said Clay had hit a field goal out of his own end zone, which was a sixty-two yarder. (The AFL field is shorter than a standard football field but the field goals are much narrower and the cross bar is higher above the ground.) Needless to say, Clay certainly had the credentials as a professional kicker. More than that, he was a great teacher.

From the moment I met him, he became a person that I could go to for advice—especially if it was related to kicking or about other aspects of football, such as recruiting. We remain in touch today.

With my mom and Andy's support, Clay began to teach me about technique and form and a host of other aspects that would help me be a better kicker and a better player. I traveled to his home in St. Louis during summers prior to the season to receive training and correction. Clay was quick to point out my flaws and show me where I was wrong. It was tough but I knew it was necessary if I wanted to be prepared once the season started.

Clay issued various workouts that I would need to do during the offseason that was added to the other conditioning I was doing with the football team. In all honesty, I owe everything I know about kicking a football to him.

The biggest misconception out there is that the kicker's job is easy, that all you need to do is head out onto the field and kick the ball. That thinking leaves out an awful lot of precision and preparation. Clay told me that I needed to be a technician, and he wasn't lying.

You must have a very focused mind to pull off a successful kick. There is a peculiar geometry to the whole process. The smallest mistake aiming or in execution can send the ball sailing wide of the goal post.

I learned a lot even in that first several months working with Clay. I took the refinements and the knowledge he provided and vastly improved the course of my eighth grade football season. I think the highlight of that year was hitting a thirty-eight-yard field goal during a game against South Vermillion. It was a memorable accomplishment, in some respects, because it was not something that usually happened in junior high football. Most teams just didn't kick field goals at that level.

I'VE GIVEN some examples already in the book about the opportunities that become possible when another person, be it a coach, a teacher, or a mentoring figure simply takes the time to see you and believe in you. For me, Clay Rush has to be one of the great players in the game called life and spared some of his time to help a kid that in whom some people saw little promise. That simple act, no matter who is involved, can change lives. I believe that and I hope I can be that for someone else.

I look at it this way: Clay went out of his way to make sure that I was doing all of the necessary work to better myself. How could I not do my very best not to disappoint a person like this? When somebody goes out of their way for you, you want to do the same.

I poured every ounce of dedication I had in those years of training. I can remember doing stretches for twenty minutes to a half-hour every night followed by 200 crunches. My flexibility increased tremendously. In fact, I was able to do the splits both ways. Flexibility is a tremendously important component in kicking. Not only does it help prevent injuries but it also gives you more control over your kicking form. You can attain a higher degree of accuracy and stability. These are both imperative and necessary if you want to pull off a successful kick. That was one element of the training; there were others. Two days a week, I would head out to the pasture at home and run up the biggest hill I could find. I did twenty sprints up followed by ten more running backwards. By the time I was finished, I could barely walk.

Clay expected a lot of me. He had a very clear philosophy concerning the role and proper expectations associated with being a kicker. Many of the players who were kickers wrongly assumed that since their job was so limited that they could afford to sit around during the practices while the other players were out training.

Clay didn't buy that. He said you needed to be out there too, working your tail off with your teammates. In truth, he said that I should be working harder than everyone else. There was justification for accepting the status quo. If you want to be good at something, if you want to be better than average, you have to put in the time. You can't settle for being content with what you've accomplished so far. I heard someone once quote that "Being good is the enemy of being great." I'm not sure who said it, but I think it says something crucial. It is a view that is not always easy to see. Many people, once they've reached a certain point, simply settle. Higher excellence is never achieved.

Let me put this in a familiar context: In many cases, kids are just content with being on the varsity team or with being a "decent" player. They scarcely dare to dream of more. They seem to shun the idea of greatness because they think it just isn't something they can achieve. They think they're good enough so they miss out on that greatness. I just don't understand that mindset. If you really want something you will go and get it no matter what it takes. It takes work, it takes commitment, and most of all it takes belief.

I identified with Clay's vision and strived to be a better kicker with such thoughts to carry me forward. I pushed my body. Following the guidelines of his workouts, I headed to the weight room. I needed to add strength and speed along with flexibility. I entered a routine to build up leg speed that included longer reps of lifting than most of the other players did. Where they might do eight or ten, I was doing twenty. By the time I was a senior in high school, I was lifting 600 pounds for twenty reps.

The work was often grueling. Single leg squats were probably the worst part for me. I remember visiting Clay and he had me do them on the bleachers at the local school. If I lost my balance or fell off, Clay would make me start over again. During the short visits I had during the summer, Clay packed a lot of training and teaching into a few days. He was always evaluating my current levels and made sure to point out areas where I could improve. It was amazing and I loved those summers. I came back to Indiana like a brand new kicker every time.

I can tell you that Clay was always pushing me beyond what I thought could be possible. He made me reconsider many things and I think this insight became crucial not only on the field but also in life in general. People often let their own expectations and points of view limit them needlessly. For someone with my circumstances, that mindset cannot take root. I know that anything is possible if I put my mind to it.

On one occasion, Clay strapped me in a harness and tied it to a vehicle and had me pull the vehicle about forty yards about five different times. When I came home I used my step-dad's truck and pulled that. A lot of people did not believe I could do it, but those who saw it were amazed. I've always had good leg strength but pulling the truck like that definitely increased it.

Whatever it was that Clay Rush saw in me that day at the Purdue camp, he truly believed. He believed in me and I will forever be thankful for the opportunity I had to train with him. I can't count the times I get into a situation and something he said or showed me comes to mind. Life lessons are often forged in the kind of relationships we have with people who have a mentoring spirit, the desire to reach out and help improve the lives of others. Those kinds of people are valuable and I have the utmost respect for those who've taken a chance on me.

"It's lack of faith that makes people afraid of meeting challenges, and I believed in myself."

—Muhammad Ali

6

Freshman Year

MOST OF you probably remember, at least a little bit, what a transition it was moving from junior high to the high school level. There were many small differences I had to absorb and get used to. The level of instruction, the assignments, the variety of classes, and for someone engaged in school athletics there were changes that came in terms of the coaches, the players, and the expectations.

I went into high school very nervous, not knowing where I fit into the social scene or what I would become. They were natural insecurities that every teenager has and things every student goes through. I was lucky enough to have a senior named Chloe Dark step in to help me get acquainted with things. She always seemed to have my back and acted like a big sister. Still, my situation was slightly different than my classmates. High school can be scary for anyone, even kids who do not have a disability. I had to draw on the confidence I had gained playing sports, the strength of will forged on the ball diamond and the playing field. I stubbornly refused to accept failure. I was going to take normal classes, even though I could take tests in a different room and take longer if I wanted. I wasn't willing to take the easier route. It was a struggle in some classes, but I did very well in others.

I had already shown myself to be a capable football kicker and I made sure that I never let anyone just assume I couldn't do something because of my arms. In football, I think I gained new opportunities to grow and develop as a kicker and an all-around player. As a freshman I was introduced to perhaps one of the toughest coaches I've had. Coach Dave Bolin was never soft on me. He had a tendency to yell a lot to get his point across and to bring home the lessons he was trying to secure on the field. He was a tough coach that demanded a lot from his players. I was treated the same as anybody else. He probably yelled at me more than anyone ever has. I couldn't stand the intensity at the time, but I believe I understand it more now. I respect what Coach Bolin was trying to do.

It is often the case that as a young player you tend to react strongly or emotionally when being challenged so much to achieve certain goals. It gets the best of some and they don't make it. They fail to grasp the essence of what the coach was trying to teach them in order to be a successful and competitive player. Those who persevere will often look back and recall the relationship with a coach fondly. They realize, in hindsight, that most coaches are simply trying to make them better athletes.

Going in as a freshman, I became acquainted with Bolin's methods and expectations and I fed them into my own burning competitive spirit. In turn, I carried in some of the lessons that Clay had been teaching me up to that point. That year was a time of rebuilding on the team even though we did have a few good players on the line up. I won the starting spot on the team during two-a-days for both field goals and kick offs. (I would have been the punter as well if the shoulder pads hadn't been in my way.)

As the season commenced, I fell into the routines of training and practices. The team trained very hard in preparation for our first regular season game. We faced South Montgomery. I remember being very nervous to kick at this level as a freshman, especially with such a demanding coach. The locker room before the game was pretty quiet and I paced back and forth a little bit, glancing down at the twenty-one emblazoned across my jersey. For his part, Coach Bolin gave a good speech to motivate us. It helped to steady my nerves some so I felt better and was ready to go. Southmont won the toss and chose to receive, which meant I was the person to start the game by kicking the ball deep to them. You would not believe what happened. They ran it all the way back—on my very first kick off ever! Needless to say, it wasn't a great start to my varsity-kicking career.

That failed kickoff was the only action I saw the entire opening game. Southmont went on to win the game. We never scored a point. The following week, Coach Bolin came to me and told me that I needed to improve my performance so I would be able to kick the ball in the end zone so the opposing team wouldn't be able to return it. It was a lesson learned and I went to work from that point on.

During the next game against Turkey Run the team played much better. I was able to kick three extra points and hit my first varsity field goal of 32 yards. We ended up winning our first game of the year. Following that game, I started getting recognition as a kicker in our area. Not very many teams kick field goals, let alone freshmen. You add the fact I was a kid with short arms and you had the right ingredients to almost guarantee that the media would take notice. Before I knew it, I had local television stations wanting to come do a story on me at practice and film me. At first, I looked at these instances as just more brushes with local celebrity added to others that had cropped up for as long as I could remember. Yet the notoriety I received as a varsity football kicker was also different. I was excelling in a sport that some would have never imagined I could have a place.

One of the immediate impacts felt on the team was how Coach Bolin reacted to all of the attention. Honestly, I knew that he really didn't like it. He just wanted to focus on playing well on the field. Additionally, I felt more pressure to do well in the games. I believed that if I was getting all of this coverage from the media then I should be focused even more on executing each aspect correctly when I kicked.

The other effect was focused on how my teammates treated me. The guys liked to mess with me, calling me names like "big time" or "Hollywood." I think I even picked up the nickname "super foot." The jesting was done in good fun and I embraced the names the same way I rejected the hurtful names that I was called in the past. I think the attention lent a festive air to the events at the time. However, we were also a team with serious goals for the season. The top one was to win a sectional championship.

While I know I'm not saying anything new or revolutionary, I feel it's always important to get back to basics. Despite the attention I was receiving, I never fooled myself into thinking I was somehow a star or that the team would suffer if I didn't grace the field with my "super foot." Football is not an individual sport—it is a team sport. You need every player to do their jobs if you want to be a successful team. As with most sports, it is true of other things in life. No matter what you can accomplish on the field or in some other venture, you will probably rely on someone else at some stage in the process.

I don't mean to say that I did not strive to be my best in light of the whole team effort. Not at all. I can't deny my nature. That competitive streak that's helped me get up when I've fallen was too strong to suppress. That drive that led me to put myself out there time and again, both on the field and off, always made people stand up and take notice.

Here's a case in point: During a game against Attica, we were up 14-7 with not much time left in the game. We just scored and I had to kick off. The return man broke free and I was the only one left to tackle him.

Without hesitation, I ran, took a good angle, and made the tackle. It was something out of the ordinary for a kicker to do—even ones with full-length arms. The crowd seemed to be very shocked by the move. As a direct result, I got Hit Of The Week for that hit as well. I received a shirt commemorating the occasion. (It is still hanging in my closet.) One of my good friends from Attica, Anthony Vredenburgh, was on that team. Later on, when I visited his house a lot, Anthony's parents liked to bring up my tackle and did so just about every time I came over.

Looking back, I could have very easily believed that there was no way I could make that tackle. I was just a freshman. Besides that, I had small arms. Such thoughts were fleeting. I simply would not accept that. I respected myself. I respected the game of football too much for that. In reality, great things only happen when you go after the things you want. You have to draw strength from whatever sources makes sense for you and you take a chance. And you keep going.

LIFE IS filled with setbacks. I'm sure many people remembered that simple truth when they saw me for the first time. I think I realized early on that I could have become defined by my disability or I could shape how people perceived me. One of the most important ways to do that is to decide beforehand how you accept setbacks when they come—as they inevitably will.

The latter part of the season was marked by some unexpected hardships within a short period of time, both for our football team and me personally. In the first case, our best player ended up getting hit extremely hard in the final game of our regular season. It took him out the rest of the season. Darrin Alexander was our running back, and since we mostly ran the ball it hurt us deeply in the sectional. We ended up barely squeaking by North Central our first game and had to face Riverton Parke in the second round.

That very same week my family had a personal tragedy. My Grandpa Rogers suffered a heart attack while he and my grandma were on vacation. Although he passed away that evening, I found some comfort in the fact that he died doing what he loved: traveling and gambling. Those who knew my grandpa best knew how much he loved to go to Las Vegas. I think it was fitting that he went out in a way that he would have wanted.

My mom tells a story about how he called her the night before and talked for a good while, which was very unusual for him. She thinks it was almost like he knew something bad was going to happen. He was a great man and did a lot for my mom and me. I know he is still looking down on me every day.

In light of my grandpa's death, Coach Bolin didn't pressure me to play at all during the sectional matches but I told him I would anyway. In the end, I don't think I helped all that much. We got shut out and knocked out of the sectional. Darrin's absence deflated our chances; we fell short of our goal. It was an opportunity that we went after with everything we had despite the troubles that seemed to get in the way. I could have sat out and dwelled on my personal loss but I chose to put myself out there. Not everyone would have made the same decision.

In the light of our loss, I think it made sense that we decided that the best thing we could do was work harder for next season. Even when life throws you a curve ball, the right attitude can take you farther than you might think.

"It's not so important who starts the game but who finishes it."

—John Wooden

7

A Season To Remember

TIME OFFERS perspective. I'm sure most of you would agree with that idea. In reporting some of the events that occurred during my early childhood up through high school, I think I've gotten some perspective and I'm able to look back on those times with a clearer eye. I hope I've offered a unique viewpoint. Someone with full-sized limbs or whose body is totally sound can't quite picture everything I'm talking about. That's okay, because despite outside differences and limitations, people experience life similarly. This is true whether you're a young person or an adult.

I think it's fair to say that my sophomore year of high school seemed like a really crazy period of time. I was growing up and assuming new responsibilities not just on the football field but also in the classroom. That year was also when I went and I got a driver's license. It was a time of changes. It was one of the most difficult football seasons I had ever had. I struggled along with my teammates through every practice, every game, so that I can say, honestly, that it was a season to remember. My thoughts naturally gravitate towards the peculiar struggles that come with high school athletics, but I experienced other things away from the field.

AFTER THE end of freshman year, I entered summer vacation knowing that I would take the driver's education program to qualify for a license. I know it may seem odd to some of you to imagine me driving at all. I was lucky enough to be in the training vehicle with two of my best friends, Rodney Carver and Justin Krout. Our instructor was Dan Halladay. To this day, I remain impressed with his courage for getting in the car with me behind the wheel. Seriously though, when I was driving he never acted worried or scared. Perhaps he had confidence that I would do what was necessary. In a way, this may have boosted my own confidence. I was nervous about the whole idea despite coming into the class with some prior driving experience. I believe I was able to drive so well because I had lived, or been around a farm, most of my life.

My grandpa always let me drive the tractor when I was little and we also lived on a gravel lane so my mom let me drive the car down the road all of the time. I count driver's ed as a success. Rodney didn't end up getting us killed and Justin only ran a couple stop signs, but we made it. Most of you are probably wondering right at this moment how I drive. I guess it is just something you have to see for yourself to understand. When people ask me how I drive, I say just like you "normal" people do. I've got to smile a little at that, but it is also an accomplishment.

As with other things, I could have just believed that driving was impossible. I could have bought into the notion that since I didn't have full-length arms that I had no business being behind the wheel of an automobile. Driving was a wonderful new privilege but it was also an opportunity that I seized with my usual determination. It was a part of my life that I definitely wanted to mention since it was life-changing in its own way. I gained a new level of independence—something that I think those without disabilities take for granted. I am more cognizant of what I achieved and appreciate that I can drive today.

Like I said, driver's ed happened before sophomore year but it definitely impacted my experiences. It was a bright spot to start off what I've already called a season to remember. I look again at football, but I want to emphasize that no matter where your area of pride and accomplishment lies, it is so important to be aware of those kinds of accomplishments. They can serve as valuable milestones that will help keep you on course as you go on to other pursuits in life.

THE SOPHOMORE year of my varsity football season will be a time I will always remember fondly. It was an incredible time for me. We knew going into the season we were a very young team. I believe we had to start about seven sophomores, which usually doesn't make a very good football team unless all of your sophomores are pretty gifted athletes. We had a few upper classmen who were seasoned pros by that point so it helped us all out.

We had an explosive start to our season, quickly moving up to 3-0. It was a rapid succession in which we beat Southmont, the team who beat us 55-0 the year before, followed by victories over Turkey Run and Riverton Parke.

I don't dispute the fact that we might have grown a bit cocky due to our early performances on the field. Maybe we walked around with our chest puffed out and our heads held high. I know that this kind of attitude can often be the precursor to disaster. One moment you're on top and then the next thing you know things start going wrong. In our case, we had a player get in trouble for partying and a couple more got into a car wreck. If you add in a few other mishaps, we were missing five of our players in a short period of time. At that point, we went on a four-game losing streak. This was a low point, one of the valleys our team had to venture into before we soared to the mountaintop, so to speak. It was perhaps the worst four weeks I've ever had as a football player.

Coach Bolin was in a decided foul mood—even for him, which was saying a lot. He ranted and raved, struggling to get us motivated to play hard and attempt to turn us back in the right direction. The loss of those players was quite a blow to those who remained and had to go out on the field.

During the four games we lost, the Mustangs only scored one touchdown. We were defeated in one game 69-0 by the eventual state champions, Seeger. Practice was beginning to become one of those things that you dreaded throughout the day. For my part, I struggled with my kick offs. The ball wasn't going into the deep right corner where Coach Bolin and my teammates surely wanted it to be. Instead it sailed out of bounds or into the middle of the field. Every time I had one of these kicks during practice the entire kick off team, including me had to do "up downs." For those of you that know what an "up down" is, you are imagining how I did them. Well, I can tell you they were not pretty.

I remember thinking, "Man, I thought I was good, now I'm causing my team to get punished for my mistakes." It was a real eye opener for me. It certainly was a lesson in the value of teamwork and how each us had an important role in our success as a group. I felt the responsibility more keenly than ever before. Despite the intensity of those practice session, I can look back on Dave Bolin with ample respect. He pushed me hard and yelled a lot. I hated it then, but love it now.

SOMETHING HAPPENED. All the hard work we put in paid off by the end of the season. We were entering the sectional and our team was back and we were ready to go in and secure a victory. We won our first two sectional games and were slated to face off against Rockville in the championship game. I was very anxious during that whole week while the team prepped for the game. I was itching to play and kick a long one right down the middle.

However, we had some unexpected setbacks. Rodney broke his collarbone so he wasn't able to play quarterback. Also, teammate Reuben Dark was injured. He was also one our best defensive players. Once the day arrived we piled aboard the bus and headed for Rockville for the sectional. Going in I wondered what kind of atmosphere there would be surrounding the competition. How would the crowds react compared to ours back home? Without Rodney and Reuben, I knew we were in for a difficult battle.

I remember Rockville starting a little better than us. I believe they took a 6-0 lead early in the game. In the second quarter we were driving down the field and got stalled on the 25-yard line. The time came when Coach Bolin called out the field goal unit. I was a little bit nervous because it was going to be a 42-yarder and as a sophomore, it was not an easy kick. I remember standing right by John Carver on the sidelines and talking to him.

I said, "I think it's too far."

He looked at me and said, "Go kick the damn thing in."

John Carver is Rodney's uncle. He was in an accident back in high school trying to stop a hay wagon from rolling down the hill. It ran him over and left him paralyzed and in a wheelchair. He has always been a strong motivation for me, especially when I hear stories of how tough he was back in the day as a wrestler. He was always there for the team during weights and practices, encouraging us to play harder. He was another one of those guys who did not take it easy on me and might have yelled at me a little more than most people. Needless to say, I went out and kicked the ball right through to put three points on the board. We got the ball back and scored a touchdown. Justin threw his first one of the year to Cole Bowman, Giving us a 10-6 lead. Rockville ended up scoring on a long touchdown right before half to give them a 12-10 lead.

Heading back to the locker room, Coach Bolin said, "Relax. We are going to win the game."

It just so happened on the opening kickoff of the second half I pinned them down in the corner and almost as if it was planned, Rockville fumbled, putting us in great field position to take the lead back and we did. Justin threw another touchdown, this time to Shad Jones. We took a 17-12 lead. The game went on without anyone scoring. With only a few minutes in the game Rockville started to drive the ball down the field. I got nervous. As they inched their way down the field, they were about to our ten or so with thirty seconds left.

Jesse Scott looked at me and said, "We may have to do something we haven't done all year, run a kick off back."

I said, "No, we are going to stop them."

Rockville ran the ball a time or two and finally it was down to one play. It was fourth down from about our ten. The quarterback rolled out and tossed the ball high into the corner of the end zone. I saw two of our guys around and thought for sure it was going to be knocked down. I saw all three of them sort of go up for it. As I stared at the field to see where the ball was I couldn't find it right away.

Who the heck came down with it? I was freaking out. Both sidelines thought they had caught it. Finally, I saw the ball rolling around on the ground. We had won! If you have ever won a big game like that in intense fashion, you know the feeling I had that day. It was an incredible sectional victory for the Mustangs.

While we did lose the regional against Linton, I can still call the season a good one, one worth remembering. I am still proud of the accomplishment.

"Always make a total effort, even when the odds are against you."

—Arnold Palmer

Me kicking the record-breaking 48 yard field goal

8

Falling Short

I CARRIED a comfortable pride with me following sophomore year. Our success winning the sectional was a badge of honor among the players. While we did not win regionals that season I still look back on us ending on a good note. Those of us returning the next year had high hopes for solidifying a larger victory. There were many expectations, those we put upon ourselves, those issued by our head coach Dave Bolin, and I think it was fair to say those of the fans too. We had played a good season. I believed that my junior year held the promise of an even better season.

During the offseason we trained and focused on our game. By the time the new school year started I was on track to become the all-state kicker that I believe Bolin wished me to be. I was very confident. I think that my fellow Mustangs were confident too. The sectional win was perhaps a big reason why we felt such renewed confidence coming into the season. We had started seven sophomores and triumphed over the Rockville Rox. Still, I had no idea what to expect. There were so many opportunities for us to succeed and to make it farther. I knew I was ready to go.

We started out fairly strong in the beginning of the season. Over the course of several weeks, we had seven games and won all but one. I was happy with the trajectory of the team; it seemed that we were on the way to achieve greater things. With the Mustangs 6-1 so far that season, I received quite a surprise when Coach Bolin came to me one day and said that I was invited to an Indianapolis Colts practice at the Colts Complex.

I had come to the attention of their placekicker, Mike Vanderjagt. I later found out that it was his golf instructor who first mentioned me to Vanderjagt. He was intrigued enough to contact Fountain Central. I was sort of shocked by the chance to visit an NFL practice. I, in turn, invited Coach Bolin and his son, Jack, to go with me.

Once we arrived, I just wanted to absorb it all. It was fascinating to see how the pros practiced and to take in sights of their amazing facilities. I had a tremendous amount of fun that day. We met and talked with Vanderjagt and also met the Colts' kick off specialist, Dave Rayner. Following the practice, Coach Tony Dungy, Payton Manning, and Marvin Harrison came over to meet me. My day was getting better by the second. They were all class acts and very generous. I can tell you truthfully I respected them even more than I already did.

After we had chatted a few minutes, everybody wanted me to lace up and kick a few balls. I was floored for a second by the request but then stepped up and gave it my best shot. It was a once-in-a-lifetime opportunity. I sure wasn't going to miss out. I didn't disappoint them. I drilled a couple of forty-yard (and over) field goals.

A local news station was there during that practice and had been following us around the whole time. I remember Vanderjagt talking with the reporter. He said he couldn't believe how I could use my balance to kick without the use of my full arms. He said I kicked a great ball. The footage was aired on the evening news. Later, at school, I was surprised when the administration aired the coverage for the entire school during the activity period held at the beginning of the day.

It was an exciting experience that I will not soon forget. Very few people get that sort of chance let alone when they are only juniors in high school. I had no idea that I would have other memorable experiences in the years ahead, more opportunities to share who I am, what I've accomplished, and how I have strived despite some physical limitations. That visit to the Colts complex was an eye-opening event that let me see into the world of professional sports.

That trip was a personal high point for me. I sort of carried my enthusiasm for a while after and was happy that our football team continued to move forward in the season. We were becoming a better team, maybe a force to reckon with, and in the end we went 8-1 in the regular season.

The season started with a series of great wins in which we defeated Southmont 42-21, followed by Turkey Run 49-7, Riverton Parke 35-0, Covington 62-6, and Attica 35-0. We had a 5-0 start when we met Seeger on the field. The team came in hot. I made a forty-two and a thirty-nine yarder during the first half. They were great kicks and made that game my best performance of the season. Unfortunately, Seeger scored touchdowns left and right. My field goals proved ineffective to dislodge their advance. Seeger won the game. We followed up our solitary defeat by taking Benton Central down the next week, followed by a victory over North Vermillion 54-14. We finished our regular season by winning against Rockville 31-0.

There was a great deal of momentum on our side. We were ascending to become one of the more dominant teams in our conference. It seemed that our hopes for the season were coming to pass. Following the game against Rockville, something happened.

I don't know exactly what it was but I do know that the team's chemistry just collapsed. I wish I had an explanation. We came out of the first round of sectionals and "laid an egg." In football terms, we came out on the field, played terribly, and just lacked focus. We played Riverton Parke, a team we had defeated 35-0 in the regular season and they simply beat us. Taking nothing away from them, they came out and just outplayed us. That's the simple truth. They claimed a 36-22 victory and we were knocked out of sectionals. Riverton Parke went on to win their first sectional ever in football. It was a huge wake up call for me.

We fell short that day. Our team had all of the skills needed to come away the sectional champs for the second year straight. At first, I felt like we had just wasted our chances out there. We had squandered the precious opportunity to come away champions. Looking back on those events from a few years down the road, I can see them more clearly and with less emotion. Setbacks happened all the time in life. Sometimes they don't mean that much; you must simply get up, wipe away the dust, and go for it again. Other times, those instances can have a profound impact on what happens later.

When we lost that game, I think something happened to Coach Bolin. Maybe his heart just wasn't in it anymore. As a coach, you want your players to come out and give everything they've got for you. In my opinion I think the team fell short; they failed to give it their all. Did I have any evidence? No, but I just felt that way. Maybe I was wrong.

Later that year, the word spread that Coach Bolin was stepping down from the head coaching position at Fountain Central. It was the beginning of a time of uncertainty for the other players and especially myself. We had no idea then who would be taking Bolin's place as the new coach. For me, as a kicker, the question raging through my mind was whether the replacement would be interested in ever kicking field goals. I was anxious, but I would have to wait like everyone else to see what my future in football would look like.

"Winning is about heart, not just legs. It's got to be in the right place."

—Lance Armstrong

9

A Leg Up On The Competition

BEFORE THE school year ended my junior year we had a football call out meeting in the cafeteria. We were introduced to our new coach, a man named Curt Trout. I remember meeting him and thinking he seemed like a good guy. I was hopeful that he was also a good coach. We would be working together during the summer to prepare for our last season of high school football. Being a senior comes with a whole assortment of hopes and expectations unique to that time of life. My mind was focused on finishing well in high school athletics. I also knew that a part of that had to do with the kind of coach we were going to have.

Looking back, there is one thing I thought Coach Trout did very well; he endeavored to build relationships with each of us. That may not seem like much to some people, but to a player there is something very special about a coach who walks that extra mile to develop good relationships with the players. The creation of trust can make a big difference when it comes time to walk out on the field. Most coaches maintain a business-like distance and focus merely on getting results in the games. They pay little attention to what really matters in life of those kids that are under their guidance. In my opinion, a coach has a duty to be a mentor to his or her players. As a coach, you could win every game and receive all the glory from the press, but if you are not willing to help change your players' lives for the better, do those wins really matter in the end?

I suppose a little age provides me with some broader perspective on the subject. A coach of quality is one who not only gets you to do the hard work necessary to achieve great things, but also does it by inspiring you to be the best you can be. Such coaches care not only what you're doing for them on the field but also how you are doing in classes and other areas of life. One aspect can affect or influence another. It takes wisdom to recognize that.

THE PROSPECT of my last season of high school football prodded me early on. I was trying to come to grips with that milestone and knew that I had to think about not only that season but also position myself so that I could have a shot at moving on and playing at the college level. I wanted to continue kicking but I knew that I needed to intensify my training.

I remember getting straight down to business for football once track ended in the beginning of the summer. We had weights three days a week with the team but I typically worked out five days a week over the summer or so. I needed to get my leg strength up so I could get my kick offs into the end zone and possibly break the school record for the longest field goal, which I was told was forty-three yards. I was also only weighing about 160 pounds at the time and Clay told me I needed to get to about 180 to have a legitimate shot at a college scholarship. This prompted me to change my diet quite a bit. I had protein shakes and peanut butter sandwiches before bed. I ended up gaining those needed twenty pounds but not all of it was muscle like I wanted.

I was training very hard, running hills, lifting with the team, pulling my step dad's truck. It was a great summer and I got much stronger and could kick the ball further than I ever had. I was hitting well over fifty yarders if I had the wind at my back. My flexibility was also great; I could do the splits both ways.

Additionally, I made the rounds at some camps hoping to get noticed by a prestigious college. I went to Purdue, Indiana, Notre Dame, and a Ball State camp all within a month's time. Of those visits, I believe I performed the best at the Purdue camp. (A touch of irony, perhaps, since I did end up going to Purdue for a time.) At the camp I hit about every kick they threw at me. A few weeks later I received a letter from the staff saying they would be keeping an eye on me to see how I did during the season. It was a nice letter, but I wasn't foolish enough to get pumped up about it unnecessarily. Colleges send thousands of those kinds of letter out each year to prospective players.

In contrast, I had an eye opening experience not that long after attending the Purdue camp. I traveled to a camp at Illinois, and kicked for one of their coaches. Without hesitation, he told me I wasn't a Division One kicker, especially not a Big Ten kicker. That little trip stuck with me and has always been a reminder that I need to keep striving. That coach just added more fuel to my inner fire to succeed.

The summer before my senior year was great. Besides the training and other activities, I received recruiting letters, the biggest obviously being from Purdue and a few smaller ones from Valparaiso, Manchester, and Franklin. I was happy enough. I knew that I wasn't exactly what you might call a *top* recruit.

WE STARTED out the season strong under Coach Trout. I learned very quickly he wasn't afraid to try long field goal attempts so I felt more at ease going forward. In fact, in the first drive of our season, during a game against Southmont, I came out in fine form. I hit a forty-eight yarder, shattering the school record for the longest field goal, and I came to find out later, also breaking the conference record. The media spread the word. It was a huge accomplishment for me, but more importantly our team started off 1-0, beating Southmont 24-0. Over the next several weeks, the Mustangs systematically defeated our opponents only losing one game in the regular season 12-7 to Seeger. Most of the games were blow outs. We beat Turkey Run 55-8, Riverton Parke 34-6, Covington 68-3, Attica 31-0, and

North Vermillion 51-13. So we had a pretty good regular season under our new coach.

Going into the sectionals we were again at 8-1. I was cautiously optimistic. We had a chance to set things right and avoid another early exit. Honestly, I think all of us hoped we would get the opportunity to make it all the way to the state championship.

We won our first two sectional games, so we had to face Riverton Parke in the sectional championship—the team who knocked us out in the first round last year after we had already beat them 35-0! We were more focused and emerged victorious as sectional champs, beating them 31-6. It was a relief.

Following the win, we were going to play Perry Central, a team from southern Indiana, a team we had never played before, in the Regionals. I remember the week preparing for Perry Central was a little different than others. It was a totally different atmosphere than I had ever experienced. Yes, we had played in a regional before, but we weren't expected to win that one our sophomore year. This year people—the fans—were expecting us to win and make the trip to semi-state the following week. We had a good week of practice even though the weather was much colder than it had been in previous weeks. Finally, game day came and it was time to see which team would advance to semi-state and play Indianapolis Ritter.

The game was a little muddy and pretty cold. I noticed the footballs were not flying as far as they normally would previously in the season. The game started out really slow. We knew they were going to try and run the ball all over us because they had an enormous line and a good running back, but our defense held pretty well. Perry Central scored and it was 7-0 at halftime. I remember thinking, "That is fine; we will score and tie it up because we get the ball first starting the third quarter."

The first drive of the quarter we tried to do a throwback screen which they read perfectly and picked it off taking it for a touchdown, making the score 14-0. It must have lighted a fire under our players because Perry Central didn't score again in regulation and we put up two touchdowns, making the game 14-14 with only a few minutes left in the game. We had the ball about mid-field, trying to get into field goal range or possibly score a touchdown. We dropped a couple passes and even tried a fade down the field to our best receiver Cole Bowman, which I thought was going to be pass interference but the flag stayed in the ref's pocket. It was third down and Coach Trout felt like the best thing to do was attempt to pick up a few more yards so I could try the game winner. We ran the ball and let the clock run down to about three seconds left. I jogged out onto the field to get my spot. It was hard to tell how far the kick was because the lines were disappearing from the mud all over the field. I knew it was somewhere between a 46-48 yarder. Perry Central's coach called a time out to try and *ice the kicker*, which I didn't mind; I liked the extra time I got to set up. Finally, it was time for me to get my dream kick, to send the Fountain Central Mustangs to semi-state for the first time in 23-24 years.

I got set, trying to get comfortable in the muddy footing. I knew I was going to have to shorten up my steps a bit so I wouldn't slip. The whistle blew and it was time to start. The snap was perfect, the hold was perfect, I did my steps right. There was no slip and I drilled the ball. After the kick, I glanced up to try and catch a peek at where the ball was going. It was heading right down the middle of the poles but I couldn't tell if it was going to make it far enough.

As the ball landed I saw our crowd going wild as if we had just won but then I saw the refs waiving that the kick had fallen just short. I about dropped to my knees I was in so much shock. The good news was we hadn't lost. The game was going into overtime.

For those of you who don't know how high school overtime works, each team gets the ball at the ten-yard line going in. If one of the team scores and the other doesn't, the team who scored wins, obviously. Well, the first overtime, we got the ball first. We scored no problem and I shook off my missed field goal and hit my extra point. It was now Perry Central's turn. We had them down to their last down. It was fourth down from the ten-yard line. They sent their running back out as a receiver and he got between our safeties and caught the tying score right under the goal post.

I couldn't believe it. We had to go into a second overtime. This time Perry Central got the ball first. Our defense did a great job and held them to a field goal. All we had to do was score a touch down and we would win the game. Our first play went for about six yards, so it was second down from about their four-yard line. We ran the ball again, getting a couple. Now it was third down from about their two. We ran again getting about one and half yards. It was now fourth down from about the half yard line.

Coach Trout got all of the seniors together and asked what we should do. Should we kick the field goal and go into a third overtime or go for the win? We all agreed go for the win. Only a half a yard separated us from moving on to semi-state. Those of us on the sideline were standing there, watching hopefully, some of us praying. We ran a belly play to our full back Eric Crowder. All I remember is Eric getting engulfed by a three hundred plus pound lineman. Our dream was over; we had lost in dramatic fashion. No state championship for us, not even a semi-state appearance. We were so close I could taste it.

THE END of my high school football career was one of those things in life you will always remember. Yes, I had failed my team, I could have done my part better and sent us to the next game, but I failed. There is almost always something valuable to be learned from failure. Never shun the defeats of the setbacks. Instead, use them as sources of motivation. On a personal level, I never want to let anyone in my life down, and if I do, I make sure that I learn from it.

In a way, I think sports saved my life. I don't think I would have had many friends or known half the people I know without sports. If I wasn't willing to jump in and try baseball as a second grader I would have probably never played football. I took a chance and seized an opportunity not knowing where it would ultimately lead.

At the end of the year I believe I received ample rewards for the hard work I put in. I received All-State, All-Conference, and All Bi-County. I made the Lafayette and Crawfordsville All Area team as well. Later on I found out I was invited to the Griddy Awards banquet.

The banquet was a great experience. All of the best players in the state were there to receive their trophies. Only two kickers from the entire state of Indiana were invited. I won the award of top kicker 1 through 3A and Ian McGarvey won the award 4 and 5A. Ian was headed to Ball State the following year with a football scholarship.

I was beginning a new chapter to my life. I had a fairly clear picture what the next step was going to be but I knew that life beyond high school was much different. Yet, I also knew myself enough to understand that I had what it took to make it in the real world.

My friends and I during senior year of high school. From left to right: Jesse Scott, Cap Quirk, Anthony Vredenburgh, Cole Bowman, Justin Krout, Rodney Carver, Me, and Thomas Robinson

"Don't let what you cannot do interfere with what you can do."

—John Wooden

10

Giving Back

I'VE TRIED to be clear at different points throughout this book where my heart lies on not only taking hold of opportunities when they arise but also being a source of opportunities for others. There is nothing more rewarding than being that agent of change or a mentor for somebody else in life, especially young people. I'm not so far removed from that age group that I can no longer recognize the impact that such people can play.

I've always jumped at the chance to help younger kids out in the realm of athletics. I've been involved in different activities over the years and continue to play an active role in shaping opportunities for students. It's been a role that has felt natural and I've relished the opportunities when they've come.

After graduating from Fountain Central High School, I wasn't necessarily seeking a way to get involved. In truth, I was thinking ahead to the fall when I would start my freshman year at Franklin College. It came as a surprise, really, when I got offered a chance to help out at a series of summer youth camps in our area. Four very well known coaches from the local region were sponsoring the camps. Among those involved was Dave Bolin, the former varsity coach from Fountain Central. He remains one of my favorite coaches to this day and was my head coach from my freshman to junior years. Then there was Coach Moore (The current athletic director at Fountain Central at the time of this writing), who had also been the head football coach at Seeger High School, Coach Brad Smith, known as something of a football genius in some circles. The final coach involved was named Coach Burpo, who was at that time a coach at Delphi. I didn't really know much about him but I had heard good things about him too.

The first camp I went to was at Seeger High School, a rival school of mine and where Coach Moore coached. The second camp was at Lafayette Jeff and had a few Purdue football players in attendance to help out as well. One of the players was Dustin Keller, now the current Tight End for the New York Jets.

The coaches set up several different stations for all of the younger kids to participate in. As you might guess, I had a station that involved kicking. For some reason kids are always fascinated about kicking a ball. Once they saw me kick off once and it traveled about sixty yards they all wanted to try. It was really fun working with them. I tried to teach the kids as much technique as possible given the constraints of the event. It was difficult for younger kids to understand why you use the side of the foot and not the toe. Soccer is honestly the best way to learn how to kick a football properly, but where I'm from hardly anyone plays the game.

AT THE end of each camp the coaches had some of the assistants like the Purdue football players and myself speak to the kids. I was scheduled to follow up Dustin Keller. He wasn't with the Jets just yet, but we knew after he left Purdue he was probably going to the NFL. He gave a fantastic speech and it then was my turn. I was nervous going up there but then I just found my focus and talked a little about my past and how I wasn't always known as the kicker from Fountain Central. I was known as the kid with short arms, but I worked really hard to get where I am and had a lot of support on the way. I was surrounded with good people and managed to hang with the right crowd, and stayed away from the "bad" crowd that could have gotten me into trouble and ruined my football career.

I would like to think I helped some of the kids, that I helped them realize anything is possible if you give it your all, and be willing to accept help when it came your way. Once the camps were over I looked back and realized then, perhaps for the first time, that I had something valuable to share with other people. My life, with all of its twists and turns, could be used to motivate and inspire. It was another aspect of giving back. Those speeches were a wonderful learning experience for me and I now considered the notion of speaking again in the future. I got a taste of giving back and I liked it.

THAT SUMMER was a welcome break, but I knew that the next phase of my athletic career was set to begin and I wanted to do the best I could to be prepared for that new set of challenges on the emotional and physical level. Academics had their place as well and I was already focusing on education in that case.

With the move to Franklin just a few months away I spent the summer training. I kept my worries at bay but they were still there simmering below the surface.

"People have always doubted whether I was good enough to play this game at this level. I thought I was and I thought I could be. What other people thought was really always irrelevant to me."

—Steve Nash

11

Franklin:
Where Do I Belong?

AFTER THE season was over it took awhile for me to recover and to forget about the loss we suffered in the Regional game. I've never denied the fact that I was affected by losses and setbacks. I'm human after all. Those are the moments that can truly help to define what sort of people we will be in life. I had already made the decision to keep striving and keep my eyes on the road ahead. There were bound to be other opportunities out there if I was willing to let go of what I couldn't control.

119

From that point forward I was still trying to figure out where I would be going to college once I graduated the following spring. I spent some time evaluating the choices available and ended up having it narrowed down to two colleges by the end of the year. The first option was Western Michigan. I remember the school sending a coach to Fountain Central to watch me kick for a bit. Afterwards, he offered me a chance to join the team as a walk-on once the pre-season camp was over.

My other option was Franklin College. Coach Mike Leonard was the head coach at Franklin and went more than out of his way to let me know he would love to have me as a Grizzly. Of the two, this treatment was refreshing and I was relieved to know that a team actually wanted me to come to them, instead of just being like, Yeah, come to our school, we might have a place for you." The enthusiasm of Coach Leonard was a big incentive for me at that point and knowing that they really wanted me was important. After talking it over with Clay and Andy, they agreed it was better to go somewhere that you are wanted.

By the time of my high school graduation, I was prepared to head out for Franklin College in the fall. I remember getting the packet in the mail that would explain the type of workouts they wanted you to do. The thing about Division Three is you go home for the entire summer, whereas at a school like Indiana State, the coaches want you on campus working out with the team five days a week for the entire summer. In other words, I was all on my own for the summer and it was up to me to stay motivated and to do the workouts they wanted you to do in preparation for the coming season. I'll admit it was tough. As many Franklin football players know, the packet said the first day we arrived at camp we would have to run sixteen 100 yard sprints, with each one required to be accomplished in less than sixteen seconds. That was something I could work on, a goal to shoot for among the other components of training I would undertake.

I HAVE to be perfectly honest with you. I wasn't completely happy with the idea of going to Franklin. I had always planned to attend a big time college and felt that perhaps I was underachieving. I think that changed once I arrived and realized college football is college football. Some of these guys could play at a bigger college but none were presented the opportunity that some other athletes were given. It was as simple as that. Talented players, the kind that could move on to the professional level, played side by side with guys who didn't have a future in the sport.

On the first day of camp I was pretty nervous. It was a combination of factors for me. I had moved away from home and started a college football camp the same day. As you can imagine, it was sort of over-whelming. I put my best foot forward, drawing on my training to make a good impression. I made it through the 16-100s and was on my way to my dorm room before I knew it. Once there, I met with some of the other players. At Franklin, nearly one out of every ten students at the school were (and are) football players, so I met a new one every time I turned around. Coincidently, I lived just down from two other freshmen players; one was a kicker and the other one a punter. I found it interesting that for a small college, we had a lot of kickers. I believe there were five of us there during the time I was there. We made the most of it and competed against one another during the practices, just to see what we could do.

One of the guys I met, Machy Magdolinos, was the returning starter from the previous season, a Warren Central graduate. I quickly realized that it could be difficult to get some playing time there because of Magdolinos' success and Coach Leonard made it very clear that if there are two players who were close to starting, he would always go with the upper classmen.

Over the course of those first few weeks, something had changed with me personally. I felt different and perhaps a little lost. Even now it is a hard feeling to explain, but I can say this much: I was way outside of my earlier comfort zones. I was trying to learn how to live on my own and to top it off I wasn't coming in as the automatic starter. These factors both had an effect on my performance and I would be the first to admit that I wasn't ready for the challenges then. The result of this was that I didn't train as hard as I should have. I didn't give it my all. Plus, the fact that I wasn't the starter frustrated me deeply.

In retrospect, I should have used those initial obstacles to spur me on and make me train that much harder to be the very best kicker I could be. For those reading this book today, that is exactly what I would tell those who may be in similar circumstances. Unfortunately, that kind of insight isn't always gained until after you fail. Don't be afraid of the failures and the mistakes. You've got to use them as fuel to burn, to get you ready to meet the next challenge head on.

My lack of motivation then could have ruined my chances of playing a role on a successful college football team. It took me awhile to realize how much work you had to put in at the college level. Most athletes do not ever figure this out and it can become one of the main reasons why most will never make it beyond high school athletics.

Despite all of the doubts I had I still managed to get in about four games as a freshmen. I accomplished several kick offs and hit a couple of extra points. I would add that we had a good mix of players, which made us an effective team and this aided the younger, less experienced players in the process. The players got it. Coach Leonard did a very good job with the program, turning it into one of the best Division Three football programs in the country. (In recent times, Franklin has remained at the top of their conference.) I had the good fortune to be a part of Coach Leonard's first conference championship at Franklin. Each of us received large and impressive championship rings. They made my hands look smaller than they already were. The Grizzlies got into the playoffs (you get in when you win your conference), the first time in several years for Franklin.

IT WAS a freshmen year that I will never forget. I made a lot of lifelong friends. But something was missing. I just knew deep down I had to try out for a Division One school or I would regret it for the rest of my life. I wouldn't rest until I did. Before the year ended, one night I decided to go home. I took a break from college. I set my sights on Purdue University and figured I would transfer there in the fall. The logic seemed sound to me, but in truth I think it was almost the worst mistake I had ever made. I didn't know it then, but I think I realize it more now that I'm looking back on it from a few years in the future. Perhaps, the most glaring facts were that I really had no clue at all whether Purdue would accept me and I wasn't sure they would take me as a walk-on for the team. You might say I took a leap of faith.

"The greatest mistake you can make in life is to continually be afraid you will make one."

—Elbert Hubbard

12
Purdue: A Wrong Turn

STEPPING OUT and just trusting that everything would work out for me the following year was a big risk. I admit that. It might not have been the best way to handle my college career but I never said I was perfect. I felt I had made a mistake at Franklin and thought that Purdue held out far more options for me at the time. The only trouble was I really had no idea whether I'd make it there. Like I said, I took a leap of faith. I didn't know anything concrete until early summer when I found out for sure that Purdue had accepted me for the coming fall semester. I breathed a sigh of relief. My risk had panned out.

I think my immediate thought upon receiving my acceptance notice was that I needed to start training so I would be in the best shape possible to attempt a walk on for the Purdue football team. I spent most of the summer back home, training for football and umpiring little league baseball games. I even coached my little brother's little league baseball team so I could keep busy. That summer went by fast.

I was facing other practical matters. I had no idea at first, where I was going to live and whether I would have someone to share the expenses. Rather than living in the dormitories, I opted for getting an apartment. I had a conversation with a buddy of mine named Jake Cook, who had played for Seeger in high school. He told me about his friend Mark Cravatt needing somewhere to live as well so I decided to ask him to get an apartment with me. Mark and I got along well so we decided to get an apartment a few miles away from the Purdue campus.

Once the school year started I immediately found out the date of the walk ons. I wanted to be ready to move quickly. According to the announcement it wasn't for a few weeks so I had time to get used to the classes and other aspects of a bigger college. One thing became clear very early on: Purdue was going to be very challenging for me.

When I walked into my biology class I saw a sprawling auditorium with about four hundred students in attendance. I was shocked by the size. The downside of this for me was that I never got the chance to have a one-on-one with the instructor. I didn't like this one bit. At Franklin, all of the teachers knew you and were more than willing to go out of their way to help you out. In these classrooms at Purdue, I was just another name on a very long attendance roster, anonymous and forgettable. This had a negative impact on my studies. (Let's just say I didn't do too hot in my first big lecture style class.) Now, I want to be clear that this wasn't my experience across the board. No, in some classes I did better; others I did worse. For example, I managed quite decently in my English class. I also did well in Communications. As I said, my performances in other classes varied but I was proud of my aptitude in English and Communications. It was an odd balance, academically, but I tried to maintain.

THE FIRST few weeks at Purdue were difficult for me. I was struggling to get use to a new set of daily facts about life on the much larger campus. My time at Franklin had only given me a taste of college life, but Purdue was so much more. I admit readily that it was very hard to stay motivated to train for the walk ons. There were plenty of people and events to distract me from what was most important. As a new student, I was meeting lots of new people, many of whom were insisting on coming over and who wanted to party all the time.

It's amazing to me how many kids head off to college and quickly get caught up in a cycle of partying that wastes their time and money. When you have your own apartment, you become a magnet for those types who want to get away from the dorms. Sometimes it is hard to say 'no' when you're the new guy, but in retrospect, it is far better to say no. I'd give that advice to anyone getting ready to go to college. Getting involved in all of that can cause more problems than it is worth. I'm not saying never hang out with your friends; you just need to learn how to balance it.

I WAS nervous when the day came to try out for the team. The walk ons were being held in the indoor facility, a place I was very familiar with because of previous camps. (It is where I met Clay.) There were two other kickers there and they were pretty good as well. Honestly, I should have looked into the situation more closely. Purdue already had two kickers on scholarship and were not really looking for another one. I remember thinking that we would be lucky if they took any of us.

I remember the first attempt I had. I drilled it right down the middle. The second attempt, right down the middle. The third attempt, same thing, right down the middle. I was doing very well. The other two were doing just as well though. By the end of the try out I thought I had a decent shot. The coach let us all know that the coaching staff would be talking it over and if we made it they would post it on the front door and probably give us a call by the following week. By the end of the week there were no phone calls. Basically, none of us made it.

Standing there, I had a terrible realization: I may never play football again. Furthermore, I may have ruined all of my chances by transferring to Purdue. I will tell you that this episode had a very negative effect on my outlook. I took a pretty hard hit and wasn't sure I would recover from it. For the rest of that year, I was pretty depressed.

I hated going around back home because each time I saw someone I knew I'd hear, "Hey, Brett. How's football, did you transfer or something?" I didn't like to explain my situation. I avoided it when and if I could. Whenever I saw a football game on television, I got angry and frustrated. I kept thinking, "That should be me out there." It was a tough time all around. I remember mowing my parents yard one day back at home, which I did most weekends because Purdue was only 35-40 minutes away. I was going along thinking to myself, "What's my next move? What do I do now?"

Then it came to me.

I ran inside the house and found my mom and told her I wanted to transfer to Indiana State later that fall. It was another move, another chance to get it right. I'd made a wrong turn by going to Purdue and I was determined to correct that error before it cost me my dream.

She was skeptical. "Are you serious? Again?"

She agreed to the move, but only after I insisted that it would be the last time that I did so and I would not transfer again. I agreed. Believe me, I had no desire to go through the process again since it meant spending more time in school than normal. Especially when not all of your credits transfer.

Franklin was too small, Purdue was too big, and I was about to find out how Indiana State fit me. I parted ways with all of my Purdue friends and was headed to ISU.

I COULD consider my sophomore year at Purdue a complete waste of time, or like the title suggests, a wrong turn. I lean toward this second term because it really wasn't a total loss. I still got to spend quality time with my friends. Cap stayed with me quite a bit, along with his girlfriend Kayleigh Kelp. John Elrod, who like Mark I met through Jake, also came over a bit. I had many good experiences at the university. They were some life experiences that helped shape me. They also helped me realize that if I wanted something I had to go through bouts of adversity and bad decisions. The lesson I learned was that you must never give up on your dreams. Even when you think your dream is over, if you give it everything you have, anything is possible. I am thankful for my time at Purdue, but I'm more thankful for finding a way back to the football field.

"The real glory is being knocked down to your knees and then coming back. That's the real glory. That's the essence of it."

—Vince Lombardi

13

ISU: The Perfect Fit

AS YOU might have guessed, transferring to Indiana State was something of a last minute decision. Still, I was very hopeful about the chance to go to a different college—one with smaller classes than Purdue had and where I once again had a chance to play at a higher level of football. It was a chance I was going to take.

During my first year at ISU, I was placed in the quads, which turned out to be very convenient for me because most of my physical education classes (My major was P.E.) was in the Arena, the building across the street. I didn't have to waste time searching for a parking spot like I was forced to more often than not at Purdue. In fact, I barely needed to drive at all. It was a great change of pace. Something also clicked inside my head when I went to ISU.

From almost the beginning, I got more focused and became a much better college student. I think I tried much harder in my classes. I wasn't sure what caused the change in attitude. Perhaps, I felt more comfortable with the environment. The size of the school seemed like a better fit for me. Then again, I suppose I was far more motivated given that I promised my mom that this was the last time I would change schools. It really was my last chance to get it right. Also, I knew several students that went to ISU. It seemed like I knew someone in every class I had. These were all factors, I think, that contributed to my changed mindset going into my junior year of college.

ABOUT A week or so after I came to campus I sought out information on how I could possibly walk on the football team. I quickly discovered some disturbing news from the assistant athletic director. I was way behind on credits. To be exact, I needed to take fifty-four credits that year just to be eligible for next season and even then I wasn't guaranteed a spot on the team. I had to make a decision, take eighteen credits both semesters and over the summer to even have the chance of trying out for the team or just giving up on my dream?

If you've been reading my story then you know this book is not about giving up. It is about overcoming life's obstacles. I had been given the choice, but I already knew what I would do. Honestly, I could do nothing else. I took the fifty-four credits that year so I could meet the demands of the school. I wasn't letting the dream die yet.

If I told you that the workload was easy or that I didn't have a few doubts creep in during those long months, then I would be lying to you. It was a lot of work, but I was strongly motivated. I couldn't tell you the number of "all-niters" I had to pull off in some of my classes. It seemed like the work was endless. Do you know what, though? I pulled it off.

By the end of the summer I was so relieved. The stress melted away and I felt proud of myself for what I had accomplished. I had pushed myself academically in ways I had never in the past. The only problem was, I had taken care of problem number one, but I had to do something else to claim a full victory. I needed to make the team.

Not only had I spent the previous year with my face in a book, but I had been away from organized football for nearly two years. I was sort of worried that I wouldn't be the same kicker that I once was. I had been training hard and working out several times a week so I was as ready as I was going to be for the try out. I remember arriving at Coach Minter's office to introduce myself. You should have seen his face when I walked through the door. I believed he looked a bit shocked when he saw me, like he expected someone completely different. This made me a little uneasy; it wasn't the reaction you wanted from a coach who was in charge of my walk on situation. We talked for a bit and he gave me the date when I could come and kick for them.

I had all of Christmas break to train back home, which I thought was perfect. I could lift weights at my old high school, run my hills, and pull the truck, and generally train in familiar surroundings. I was relieved I still had a little over a month to train. When I went home for Christmas that's exactly what I did. All of my friends were home. Though I was concerned they might be a source of distraction, I managed to train as much as I could and still have fun with them. I also called Clay to tell him my intentions and he gave me some ideas to help my training. It was good to talk to him. I hadn't spoken to Clay since I left Franklin. You know the feeling, when you respect someone that has helped you so much and you feel like a disappointment; that was how I felt then—like I let him down.

After the break, I was ready to make up for lost time. When I got back to school it was time for a try out during spring ball. I had to go and watch practice and kick for a few coaches afterward so they could see what I could do. That first practice ended and I was ready to go. I hit most of my kicks, as I remember, and the few coaches who watched seemed impressed. They told me to come back tomorrow and do the same thing, so I did. The next day I kicked after practice again, this time only one coach watched as I kicked twice. Then he went inside. I was really confused and worried. Did I make it? Was I on the team?

Walking into the locker room I remember seeing Bob, our equipment manager who had been there for years. He approached me and asked what size jersey I wore. It happened. I made it. I was finally going to play football again, and for a higher level than I had ever been a part of. I officially joined the team for spring ball and while I was certainly rusty, I managed to stay on the team. The weight coaches took a strong interest in helping me train. They showed me how to work my upper body, which was encouraging because I was tired of only lifting with my legs. They did a fantastic job helping me out.

After a while, I started drawing some publicity. WTHI, a local news station based in Terre Haute, Indiana, came by one practice and saw me kicking. The station decided they wanted to do a small story on me later that night. I sat and watched the clip when it aired. It was a decent clip. I had no idea what impact this small television story would have for me. I was about to be introduced to a wider world and, let me tell you, I received one of the biggest opportunities in my life, perhaps, a once in a life time experience.

"The highest compliment you can pay me is to say that I work hard every day, that I never dog it."

—Wayne Gretzky

Left to right: Sean Payton, Samantha Schroeder, my mom, me, and Dr. Phil

14
The Big Surprise

I HAD no expectations about the local media attention I was getting at ISU. I had been in the news before during high school. I wasn't a stranger to the kind of interest that many people had in someone with my physical disablities doing the things that I was doing. Simply being on the football field at all was an amazing accomplishment. I certainly did not expect what happened after that clip aired.

I found out later that that local television story had been aggregated to other media outlets across the country and ultimately attracted the notice of national television and some regional radio stations. It was a tremendous thing to consider. I was initially clueless.

About a week after the broadcast, I remember sitting in my little room in the quads at ISU when I received an email from Ace Hunt, programs director of athletic media relations, explaining that *The Dr. Phil Show* had contacted the school and asked if I would be a guest on the show. They were putting together a program on young athletes that had overcome various obstacles. It was titled "Driven To Succeed." Apparently, they had seen the WTHI footage of my practice which had spread across the web to become a headline on AOL.com. I was totally shocked. Mr. Hunt gave me an opportunity to make a final decision and then call him back. I was so excited. The first thing that I did was call my mom to tell her the news. She was absolutely thrilled about the prospect.

Around the same time, I was contacted by *Inside Edition*. The program also wanted a chance to inteview me and have me on the broadcast. Faced with a decision, I informed Ace, who said that they wanted exclusivity on my story. I ended up choosing the Dr. Phil Show.

There was some preparation involved but not as much as I thought. Not long after I accepted the invitation, other producers from the show called me and did interviews and asked me to send them pictures or videos.

Other questions followed, which oddly enough had to do with the New Orleans Saints. At the time, I couldn't figure out why they wanted to know what my opinion was of Coach Sean Payton. I thought maybe they figured since I was from Indiana that I was a diehard Indianapolis Colts fan. This happened at about the time the Saints had just beaten the Colts in the Super Bowl.

I replied that I thought he was a great coach and he did a wonderful job turning the team around after Katrina. Even after the questions, I was clueless. This happened on Wednesday and they wanted me to fly out to Los Angeles the following Tuesday. In the meantime, they were sending people to ISU to do some footage of me after our blue and white scrimmage on that Saturday. (For those of you that saw the episode, you might have noticed during a preview before I took the stage that included me talking in our locker room.)

Tuesday came and my mother, Samantha (my girlfriend at the time), and I were flying to Los Angeles. I remember being so excited on the airplane. I just couldn't believe I was going to be on the Dr. Phil Show the next day. I was used to pressure, I had kicked in front of thousands of people before. Still, this was a little different. I was stepping on to a national stage. I had questions. I was nervous. What would they ask me?

What if I didn't know how to answer a question? Would I freeze? I tried to put these thoughts aside and just bask in the excitement of the moment. I just sat back and tried to enjoy the flight.

I have to say that landing at L-A-X was an amazing experience. The airport was enormous. The descent itself had given me an unforgettable view of Los Angeles, a city I had only ever seen on television. We were lucky enough to have a driver that took us to our hotel and to the studio the next day. I don't think we could have navigated that sprawling city on our own; we would have likely gotten lost. That night at the hotel I couldn't sleep. The producers for the show wanted us awake by at least 6 a.m., but I just couldn't fall asleep. I rolled around for a few hours just thinking of how the show would go and what every one would think.

In the morning our driver arrived to pick us up a little before seven in the morning. He drove us directly to Paramount Studios. The three of us were escorted to my dressing room. We eventually took turns going through wardrobe, hair, and, yes, even make up. There we waited while the taping proceeded. I remember it feeling like days had passed before they called me out. I was just sitting there, very anxious. Finally, someone came in and said, "Okay, you're up."

I had to stand right outside the stage for a minute while they played a video of me, explaining to people why I was there. It was mainly all about my football career and goals. Then I heard Dr. Phil say, "Brett's here today, come on out."

As I walked out I saw three chairs on the stage. The one on the right had Dr. Phil in it. The middle one was empty, and in the left chair was Sean Payton. In my shock, I made the connection back to why they had been asking me about him and the Saints. The studio audience applauded and I found where my mom and Samantha were sitting. It took a few seconds to adjust to the lights, the cameras, and the whole experience.

The show went really well.

Coach Payton explained how important it is to have that drive inside of you to get where you need to go. He also surprised me with tickets to a Saints game of my choice and to stand on the sidelines for the pre game. The Colts also fired back with game tickets to a home game of my choice where I was the "twelfth man fan" of the game. I would come out to the middle of the field and be introduced over the big screen.

ALL THIS had happened during spring ball before the season even began at ISU. I had gotten some attention from papers and Indiana news stations before, but never anything like this in high school or my previous college, Franklin. I was contacted by a Canadian radio station and interviewed. So much had happened but most of it occurred during a relatively short period of time.

With all of the local fanfare that built up around my appearance on the Dr. Phil show, I remember plenty of write ups in the newspapers and subsequent television clips. It made for an eventful start to my time at Indiana State. The fact that I was being asked to speak to groups at schools was a big deal for me since I was increasingly interested in being a motivational speaker. My physical shortcomings had never been a reason to impose limitations on myself, and now I had shared my experiences with millions of people.

Let me be clear, I had no illusions that I was suddenly this big celebrity. No, I think that trip to California expanded my vision and helped to solidify what I already felt I needed to do. I wanted to give others opportunities—not only to recognize their own potential but also be willing to do the same for others.

I took this to heart, knowing I had glimpsed a possible future, and then focused on the path I had chosen. I was going to kick for the Sycamores and I was going to finish my college education. When the time was right, I would pursue being a speaker.

"Things turn out best for the people who make the best of the way things turn out."

—John Wooden

Taken on the sidelines of a New Orleans Saints game.
From left to right: Andy (my stepdad), Cap, me, Coach Sean
Payton, and Bob Campbell

15

New Orleans

AFTER THE Dr. Phil show aired I knew I had to finish the season strong before I even thought about going to New Orleans to watch the Saints play. As I mentioned at the beginning of the book ISU had one of its best seasons in years. I got the opportunity to kick in a few scrimmages and against South Dakota State. The team's ultimate goal was to win the conference so we could make it into the playoffs, but we fell a little short; losing to Northern Iowa and North Dakota State really hurt our chances. Overall, playing with the Sycamores was a great experience for me and my teammates certainly made me feel at home and a part of their football family. I have to wonder how many colleges would have been as willing to do so. I had gone as far as I could playing football and I was very happy with the results. It was the end of a long road.

WITH MY final season over, I still wanted to take advantage of the opportunity to attend a New Orleans Saints game. While they still had a few games left, the only one I could go to was the very last one at home against the Tampa Bay Buccaneers.

The Saints trip happened to be planned on New Year's—which I thought was really amazing since our hotel was right along Bourbon Street. I would be able to experience what it was like during the festive occasion. I had asked my stepfather Andy and my friend Cap to travel with me. (Andy had his friend Bob Campbell come along for the ride.) Our flight was extremely bumpy so it was a good thing I wasn't afraid of flying. Once we arrived in New Orleans, were were caught up in the traffic and crowds that had gathered in and around the French Quarter for New Year's Eve. It took our driver quite a while to get us close enough to our hotel so we could walk there. We finally made it and got changed.. We spent that night walking down Bourbon Street. I couldn't have asked for a better start to the trip. We couldn't stay out too late though, since we were scheduled to head to the Saints practice facility the next morning.

Once we arrived there, a man named Nick Karl was there to greet us. He did a fabulous job showing us around. We got to see the locker room and we were able to hold the Lombardi trophy the team had won the previous year after they beat the Colts in the Super Bowl. It was a very memorable moment standing on the sidelines watching the Saints practice. After awhile Coach Payton came over and talked for a bit to see how I was doing and then Drew Brees came over to share some words. (We were introduced to other players as well.)

After the practice concluded, we took some pictures and then headed back to our hotel. Later that night, our little group decided to go listen to some jazz at some of the local restaurants. New Orleans had some of the best jazz bands I had ever heard. Later that night when I got back to the hotel Andy and I decided to go walk around the hotel to see if we could spot anybody since the Saints were staying in the same hotel. They stay in hotels to help keep people out of trouble, even on home games. I only spotted a few players. We made our way to the hotel lounge. Once seated, we noticed Brad Nessler sitting at a table nearby. He was there to do the

Sugar Bowl in a few days so we went over and talked to him.

You may have heard his voice before; he announces a lot of college games, including basketball. He is one of the voices on the NCAA football video game. We sat and talked for hours. It was unreal that a man like this would sit and talk to me. He was very generous with his time and I deeply appreciated it. Mr. Nessler had many kind words to say. He seemed to be a down-to-earth kind of guy, something you might not expect from a celebrity. It's great when you have a lot of money or fame but you remain humble. I loved it; it was one of the many highlights of the trip.

The game was held the following day. We were allowed to stand on the sidelines for the pre-game. We saw a lot of interesting people walking around, such as Jimmy Buffet. Coach Payton came over right before the game started and took a picture that they put on the Saints' website. It was a surreal experience. It made me realize how much I loved football and how much it had done for me in my life. I felt gratitude for all of the great people that are involved in the sport as well. Although the Saints lost the game, it didn't matter. They were already in the playoffs. I came back home with a lot of great memories and shared the story with everyone I knew. Now I'm sharing it with those reading this book. I have to say that the New Orleans Saints were a real class act. I will never forget that truly unique opportunity.

I HAVE to add a final note about the offer I received from the Indianapolis Colts at the same time Coach Payton gave me a chance to attend a game. The Colts gave me the opportunity to be the "Twelfth Man" at a home game of my choice. When it came time to choose I decided to go when they were playing the Dallas Cowboys. I chose to take my little brother Drew and my friend Rodney since he was a big Cowboys fan. As with the Saints game, we were allowed to stand on the sidelines during warm ups. I was also privileged to be introduced to the whole stadium via the jumbo-tron just before the start of the game. I had a fun time there too.

Looking back, I can hardly believe that all of those events happened in such a short period of time. I felt honored to be given such gifts. There was nothing special about me. I had done nothing to deserve them other than being true to myself. Maybe that is worthy of such honor; I don't know.

Me with my little brother Drew

"Losers quit when they're tired. Winners quit when they've won."

—Author Unkown

16

On Course

THE OPPORTUNITIES I have had to meet celebrities like Dr. Phil, Sean Payton, Tony Dungee, and pro football players are priceless and they have given me experiences that few people get to have during their lifetimes. I appreciate how lucky I've been. There is a certain amount of pride in the fact, but I didn't let this go to my head. All of the attention was nice; don't get me wrong. I had friends and acquaintances cheering me on and congratulating me. When I stepped foot on that stage in Los Angeles, I had a whole studio audience applauding my fortitude and determination. Maybe millions of viewers across the country learning about my story.

Following the excitement of that period, I carried on with my college classes and studied hard. When all was said and done, one of my main goals was to be a successful football coach in my own right. If I wanted to accomplish that goal, I would have to stay focused on classwork, earn a degree in physical education, and finish up by spending some time in the field by student teaching. I had set a course and was determined to do it.

I remember talking to Andy about the prospect of getting some coaching experience. I was four classes from finishing up at ISU and knew the next step would be to complete several weeks of student teaching followed by a final test to be certified as a teacher. I wanted first-hand experience coaching but knew it might be a good idea to coach a team in a place where I didn't know anyone and where I could make some contacts that could be helpful in the future. We both thought that helping somewhere in Terre Haute might be a good place to start.

I won't lie. I was a little worried at first. I was going to contact a head coach at one of the schools in the area. I didn't know any of them at all. I was nervous but didn't let the uncertainty stop me from trying it anyway. What could it hurt after all. The worse thing the coach could say was 'no.'

I looked up Coach Jeff Cobb's email address and sent him a message, saying I would like to help out in any way so I could get some experience. To my surprise he accepted and the following week I was off to West Vigo to help out. I found out quickly it was going to be a tough year when I heard we only had two starters returning on offense. A series of coaches meetings were held simply to figure out who should play in what position. I learned a lot during my time there, especially when it came to managing a situation where you, as a coach, are short on players and have to play most of them on offense, defense, and special teams. I remember that there were certain players who never left the field during the entire game.

I found that it was easier to find my place on the team than I imagined. I worked with Nathan Gregg (the kicker), of course, and helped Jared Modesitt with special teams. Jared was the lineman coach and never coached special teams before. Since all I ever did in games was special teams he asked me to help him out a bit. We became friends during that year. I also helped Lucas Mackey with receivers and defensive backs. Even though our team ended the season 4-6, I have to say that my time at West Vigo was something I will never forget. The players became a family to me. It was a rough year but I couldn't have asked for better effort out of most of them. I gained priceless experience as a coach. For that, I have nothing but gratitude for Jeff Cobb, the coaching staff, and the players.

Following my stint at West Vigo I finished the regular coursework at ISU and knew the next step was student teaching. During the first eight weeks I ended up teaching at Covington High School in Covington, Indiana. I was under the guidance of P.E. teacher and head baseball coach, Brad Short. I have to say that I think we learned a lot from one another during those eight weeks. I gained valuable insights into what it was like to be a teacher. Plus, I had fun getting to know some of the students and made some friends among the staff. I was then off to teach at Southeast Fountain Elementary, a school I attended as a child, during the last eight weeks of student teaching. My host teachers were Mrs. Fruits, my former elementary P.E. teacher, and Mrs. Woodrow. It was great to interact with them on a peer level.

These were steps on the path. I was headed in the right direction and doing well. I know there will be more to do and I will be making important choices about employment. As this book is finishing up I have to say that I look forward to new opportunities and am

ready to meet them head on and with that same fortitude and willingness to overcome obstacles that have
characterized my journey through life so far.

"I've failed over and over in my life, and that is why I succeed."

—Michael Jordan

Taken just before we headed off to the Griddy Awards.
Left to right: Andy, Drew, me, and my mom

17
What's Next

THIS BOOK, *Kicking The Odds*, has given you a good look at my life. As you can see I have had some amazing opportunities so far in my life. Everything from playing college football to getting the chance to meet NFL coaches and players, and of course being on the Dr. Phil show; none of this would have happened if I had chosen not to trust myself, if I hadn't taken a leap into the unknown at a very young age.

I finished my high school career with several athletic accomplishments that anyone would be proud to list: I was part of two sectional championships in football, one sectional championship in baseball, and a conference championship in track. This is amazing considering that many people go their entire athletic careers without winning a single sectional.

I made All-State, All-Conference, and All Bi-County in football and also made a few different all-area teams and was lucky enough to be asked to the Griddy Awards held at the Colts Complex in Indianapolis. I broke Fountain Central's school record with a 48 yard field goal.

From high school, I was lucky enough to be a part of two different college football programs, Franklin and Indiana State—and was lucky enough to be a part of a conference championship at Franklin. The experiences and insights I gathered from those college programs will certainly be useful in the future, particularly since my aim remains to coach at the college level. You might say that all of these accomplishments were equal measures of determination, training, and even a curious twist of luck here and there. All of these elements certainly had their roles in the past.

The route I chose to get to this point wasn't exactly planned. I almost ruined all of my chances but I put my foot down and got where I needed to be. If you want something you will do whatever it takes to get it and I truly believe that. If I had listened to the hundreds of people who had made fun of me in the past, I would have never left my house. It would have been a very lonely life. I am proud of what I've become and I'm thankful for all of the support I have had along the way. I know that without those countless people who had given me simple opportunities, I would not have the prospects I have now and my future would be an entirely different one. I am not through yet. *Kicking The Odds* is only part of the story. I have future stories to tell and further chapters to write.

So what's next? If I had to put down my aspirations in a few words, I think it would be safe to begin by saying that I will be coaching for the rest of my life. That is something I am passionate about and I know I have what it takes to make it. No matter what level, be it college or high school, I will give my all in the pursuit of athletic excellence and seek to instill those core principals in every player. I will do my very best to help my future players grow to be better people in life, not just on the football field.

Beyond sports, I want to give back to the communities and use my experiences to help other people deal with their problems or overcome their obstacles in constructive ways. If I were to say I had a calling in life, I think it would be to use my circumstances of life to inspire others to go beyond what they think is possible, to strive for excellence, and never let their shortcomings deter them from what they want. To that end, I have in mind to become a motivational speaker so I can hopefully inspire others. The process of bringing this book to life has helped me confirm that desire.

Stick around folks. I am only getting started.

About The Authors

BRETT SHELDON graduated from Indiana State University with a degree in physical education. An aspiring motivational speaker, his goal is to share his insights about life with a physical disability and the role of sports in shaping his experiences with others.

SHAUN C. KILGORE is the author of numerous books including *Heaven's Point Guard: The Kirk Gentrup Story* and *Remember The Ride: The Story Of North Vermillion Girls Basketball's Sensational Four-Year Run*. He is also a freelance writer with six years of experience writing for the web. Visit *www.shaunkilgore.com* for more information.

Made in the USA
Charleston, SC
10 May 2012